PROFESSIONAL BUDO

Ethics, Chivalry, and the Samurai code

George A. Katchmer, Jr.

Publisher's Cataloging in Publication
(Prepared by Quality Books Inc.)

Katchmer, George A., 1948-
   Professional budo : ethics, chivalry and the samurai code / by
George A. Katchmer, Jr.
   p. cm.
   Preassigned LCCN: 95-060694
   ISBN 0-940871-31-9

   1. Ethics, Comparative. 2. Chivalry. 3. Bushido. I. Title.
BJ69.K37 1995   170
                                                QBI95-20148

© YMAA Publication Center, 1995

First Printing 1995

3

Printed in the USA

YMAA Publication Center
Yang's Martial Arts Association (YMAA)

38 Hyde Park Avenue • Jamaica Plain, MA 02130
(800) 669-8892

DEDICATION

To Holly, Peter, Brian, Nicky — and Ming

Acknowledgements

Once again I would like to thank Dr. Yang Jwing-Ming, David Ripianzi, Andrew Murray, and the staff of YMAA Publication Center for permitting me to foist my ideas on the public. Their patience, good-humor, and encouragement are greatly appreciated, and again I thank Chris Bernard for typing the manuscript; this time punctuated with a few laughs. A belated thank you to Dr. Thomas G. Gutheil for his thoughtful forward to my previous book, *The Tao of Bioenergetics*. As always I honor my sensei, Master Hiroshi Tajima. Finally, I want to acknowledge Matt Heck, David Franceschelli and the staff of the Montgomery County Prosecutor's Office for keeping somebody like me gainfully employed. I appreciate your forbearance — and the strange sense of humor you must have.

Foreword

Inside the entrance to the Buddhist temple that I attend is a wooden frame with two carved Chinese characters: *Wa* and *Jyun*. The word *wa* by itself is defined as the sum total, peace, harmony, unity or serenity. *Jyun* has the simple definition of order or turn. In the context of the word *wa jyun*, *jyun* has a deeper meaning; a hierarchy of values, of ethical options, or a priority of sequence of natural order, or, a duty or obligation to parents, family members, to one's fellow human beings and the environment that surrounds us in order to maintain harmony and order in our society. I contemplate the meaning of *wa jyun* and how these definitions affect my life as a lawyer, a judge, and as a person.

Comes now George A. Katchmer, Jr., the author of *Professional Budo*, with an argument "against a system of unquestioned and rigid external rules in favor of the internally generated ideas of virtue and strength." He proposes that "If we recognize the inherence of conflict in our lives, especially our professional lives, then it becomes more understandable that we take standard for our behavior from those who have made a profession of conflict — the warriors." He proposes a unique approach to that universal and eternal problem, and reasons that "since conflict is the basis of ethics, a profession that constantly studies, prepares for and engages in conflict would be the most direct appropriate model for ethics."

In my twenty-six years as a judge in Hawaii, I have seen and experienced conflict. Each conflict was polarized by parties and their attorneys, and there were as many combinations and variations of conflicts as their were litigants. The court's dilemma is to make rulings on the diametrically opposed arguments and find the correct application of the law based on the facts presented in the case.

It has been my experience and my observation that no matter how complicated the conflicts, no matter how difficult the issues, the lawyers who were well-prepared had the poise and confidence to meet any challenge. They were sure of their skills. Such lawyers got the kind of results that satisfied their clients. On the other hand, those lawyers who did not know their cases, who could not develop or refine their techniques, who agonized in making decisions, who lacked self-confidence, often fell by the wayside.

It behooves every professional to develop mental toughness, either through martial training or other disciplines. It is in the best interest of the professional to learn to resolve conflicts and live by their decisions. Those who do will prevail in the hectic world of the professional.

From the Japan of eight hundred years ago, when the way of the samurai flourished, comes the story of a famous resolution of conflict between father and son. Lord Shigemori Taira was asked by his father to lead his army in a rebellion against the Emperor. In response, he first acknowledged that the debts and obligations he owed his father were higher than the tallest mountain. And then he recited this poem:

> *"If to kin I am to be true, then*
> *disloyal to the Throne I would be;*
> *If loyal to the Throne, then*
> *untrue to kin I must be."*

and proceeded to fight for the Emperor.

Judge Frank T. Takao
First Circuit Court
First Judicial Circuit
State of Hawaii (Retired)

Preface

Welcome to the Later Roman Empire. The government is totally removed and out of control. The Huns and the Goths are sacking the countryside, and in the cities, crime, disease, and corruption are rampant. Gambling passes for economics and loveless perversion of every sort for entertainment. In response, bizarre religious sects persecute each other over fine points of doctrine. How does one live in such a world? The fact is, however, that human beings did. They survived the anarchy of a collapsed government, the terror of the Dark Ages, and later, the Great Plague, the Hundred Years War, and the Mongol Invasion. The question, again, is how?

When one cannot count on the external; governments, laws, institutions, one necessarily must fall back on oneself. In all of the times we have mentioned, this involved reliance on a personal and individual faith or philosophy of life. Unfortunately, in our present age, since World War II, at any rate, the affluence and material comforts of our society have served to close us off from the inner life and internal resources that are basic to our nature as human beings. This book is an attempt to point back in that direction. This, of course, is nothing new in itself. However, the attempt to base personal strength and ethics in our biology and in the biological energy called Qi in China and orgone by Wilhelm Reich, will, I think, give this view a stronger root than the more impersonal and bloodless dictates that pass for morality these days. You will not find a list of "Thou shalts" and "Thou shalt nots" in this book. Hopefully, you will find a great deal of good faith.

George A. Katchmer, Jr.
Dayton, Ohio
January, 1995

Table of Contents

Introduction

When I was in law school we were required to take a course in professional ethics. That it was for only one and a half credits in the entire curriculum of my legal education speaks volumes. Several years after law school, as I was well into my legal practice, the State of Ohio began to require attorneys to complete a prescribed number of hours of continuing legal education bi-annually. Again, one and a half credits of professional ethics was required. Along with the credits in ethics, however, were now included required credits in substance abuse education. This also speaks volumes.

Legal ethics, of which I can speak, but probably also other "codes" of professional conduct, such as medical ethics, are not quite what the general public envisions when they conceive of the term "ethics." Legal ethics are not some set of "thou shalts" and "thou shalt nots." They are actually a very small number of what are called "canons." These canons are generalized principles of behavior, but are really so general as to be of very little practical help.

It is true that the canons of ethics are fleshed out by so-called Disciplinary Rules, but, except in a small number of specific instances the Disciplinary Rules are about as much guidance to the practitioner as the general canons. Finally, to top it all off and add to the confusion, are the so-called "Ethical Considerations." Note that these are "considerations," not rules or positive law.

The composition of the various Codes of Professional Responsibility, however, is not due to some sort of laxness or weaseling by the various professions involved. The canons of ethics are not as broad and vague as they are due to any bad faith or desire to avoid censure by the legal, medical, or other professional communities. The simple fact is that the practice of a profession is so unique, so unbelievably broad in the situations confronting a practitioner, that our guidelines must be so correspondingly broad as to be able to encompass all that walks, hobbles, or limps into our consulting rooms.

A good deal of law school is taken up in legal theory. Many bemoan this and demand a more practical, nuts and bolts approach. However, such demands are unrealistic. There's no way to prepare one for the exigencies of professional practice than to teach one to "think like a lawyer" as Professor Kingsfield proclaimed in the movie *Paper Chase.* Again, it is not unreasonable to suspect that the same principle applies to medical and other professional education. In the last analysis, as professionals, we are on our own.

When I began thinking about writing a book on professional ethics, I, being a lawyer, naturally had the legal profession in mind. At that time I was what was termed a "docket attorney" with the Montgomery County, Ohio Prosecutor's Office. A docket attorney is a trial attorney. I was then in the middle of what would be two years of back-to-back "hell dockets," that is, courts in which there were very few plea bargains and in which most criminal cases went to full jury trials. It got to where doing two trials a week — not to mention docket calls and the assorted hearings necessary in criminal practice — was not at all unusual. I learned to prepare a credible trial in an afternoon.

During this period, in which every conceivable legal and psychological trick and means of maneuvering and deception was practiced on or by me in a court of law, it struck me that the ethics we were taught in law school were a polite joke at best. In fact, what would be more applicable would be the Code of the West, the law west of the Pecos as I used to joke in the hallways of the courthouse, or the code of conduct of the medieval samurai.

When I started preparing this book, it was to the samurai that I turned. I also pursued the instructions given under the Code of Chivalry in the West. What I found there, combined with my knowledge of other Asian practices, such as *Qi Gong* and the martial arts, and, the bioenergetic researches of Wilhelm Reich and other depth psychologists, led me to the conclusion that a set of "rules" of professional behavior was not feasible. Instead, the professional, and, indeed anyone, would be better served to look inward and cultivate the bioenergetic virtues within oneself as proclaimed by the Chinese sages, most notably Confucius and Mencius, but also by the Taoists, than to expect guidance from a source from which no guidance can possibly come.

The discussion in this book will proceed from the nature of human being in the first chapter; an academic but necessary foundation for what follows, to a discussion of *Ming* or fate in the second. This term "fate" is actually a shorthand for the nature of the world we must live in according to Confucian thought. Its exploration is the basis of all of the virtues. Ethics will be seen as necessarily derived from conflict and life will be seen as defined as conflict and struggle. In the third chapter, virtue itself, as a biosexual form of energy is examined. The practice of *Qi Gong*, or energy manipulation, is seen as essential to the increase of virtue. Chapter Four is the study of the codes of the professionals who are most intimately concerned with conflict, the samurai and the knights of medieval Europe. Finally, in Chapter Five, the attitudes of the professional warrior class will be applied to professional life in general.

I use the term "attitudes" because we shall find, as I suspected in law school, that there are no rules in life, professional or otherwise. There are simply attitudes. Good faith or bad faith. Human life is a series of questions and puzzles; Zen *koans*. Answers come when human life is completed and not before.

CHAPTER ONE

Ethics and the Human Being

A few years ago I started bleeding from one of my bodily orifices. Not my favorite orifice, but one of the better ones nonetheless. I had had an ulcer since my first year of law school, but I had never actually seen any blood. Now I did.

I am Eastern European by ancestry, so I reacted like any other person with my ethnic background would: I panicked. Then — and there's the Eastern European twist — I got morbid. I imagined myself getting thin, my hair falling out, my wife crying on *60 Minutes*. It was great fun for a day or so. We Eastern Europeans have an expression we use when we don't want to face something, it goes: "With any luck, I'll be dead by then." That's the kind of blokes we are. You have to be Polish, Slovak, or Russian to laugh at that one. It just scares normal people.

After three or four days of this delightful diversion, I called my doctor to set up an examination. I got an emergency appointment that day. My doctor, an internist, did all sorts of wonderful doctor-things, including the personal favorite of males over forty — the prostate exam. The doctor held forth on all of the possibilities involved in my bleeding while she was so engaged. My end of the conversation was less than sparkling.

With a smart snap of her rubber glove, she announced that I would have to be "scoped" and, for my further enjoyment, she was ordering a barium enema. What profound joy. The "procedures" were scheduled for the following Wednesday. With any luck, I'd be dead by then.

The night before the, uh, "procedures," was taken up

with what we will euphemistically call a ritual cleansing. I am convinced that this ceremonial drinking of the laxative has no real medical value, but is simply a practical joke developed by doctors to give them a few laughs at their professional gatherings.

"You'll never guess who I got to drink a bottle of laxative, Jones old man."

"Dear me, not that old prank. Who, Merriweather?"

"The governor!"

Peals of Hippocratic laughter.

At any rate, I drank the stuff with predictable results. I ate no food. I drank no liquid. I had no sleep — just to be consistent.

Wednesday arrived. I wasn't dead, damn it. I arrived at the doctor's office at 9:00. Everyone was smiling. They had a lawyer to torture that morning. They began with personal humiliation — the dreaded paper gown. Then they put me in a holding cell. It had damp bricks and a barred window above eye-level. Leg irons and manacles were strewn about the floor. An occasional scream came from down the hall. This was not good.

Now when my doctor, let's call her Dr. Garcia, described the "procedure" to me, she said that they would "merely be inserting a flexible fiberoptic device" into the first part of my colon. Fiberoptics, hum? I had seen these things on TV. Why, the phone company had them. They were these thin, thin, thin as a thread, highly flexible, space-age plastic things. I was a man. I could handle this thin (emphasis on thin) and flexible space-age miracle in Deep Space Nine. I should have been tipped off when I heard Dr. Garcia and her nurse guffawing behind closed doors as I gave my insurance number to the receptionist.

During the Inquisition, it was etiquette for the Master Torturer to display the instruments to be used to the condemned before the, uh, "procedure" began. This gave the evil heretic a chance to recant his errors before the fun began.

"And here we have the iron maiden, cat of ninetails, thumbscrews, rack."

"Nice rack. How much you get it for?"

"I got a brother-in-law. He gave me a deal."

Yeah?"

"You want one? What are you, a size six? I'll call my brother-in-law."

"Thanks."

At any rate, the thin, thin, thin and flexible fiberoptic "device" was a garden hose with a periscope. I saw it and instantly recanted all of my errors, both theological and personal. I confessed the Pope of Rome as my spiritual father. I gave names of friends, associates, and family members. It was not enough.

The nurse came in. She was blonde, blue-eyed, athletic. Her name was Ilse. She an SS tattoo. She stared at me cowering in my paper gown. Then the Doktor arrived.

"Zince you are a lawyer I must inform you zat zere are certain, uh, dangers involved with this, uh, procedure. In order to inzert the, uh, device, uh, I must puff air into your colon. One false move on my part and your colon could explode. You are a lawyer, right?"

"No! No! That's a vicious lie!"

It says on your chart, Herr Katchmer, zat you are a lawyer. No?"

"Okay! Okay! I also missed mass for three years. I don't root for Notre Dame. I confess! I confess!"

"Zere, zere now, Herr Katchmer. Relax. Now, shall we proceed? Assume ze position."

The horror began in earnest.

"Why are you zo tense, Herr Katchmer?" (She did actually say this.)

"I say, I really don't know old bean, perhaps it's the garden hose in my entrails. Devilishly uncomfortable, you know. Carry on. Let's have gin paheets at the Club afterwards."

"I hate gin paheets."

Of all the fun I had that day, one moment sticks out in my mind. I was laying on my side, trying not to be tense. I looked over my shoulder and there was my doctor, this attractive Filipino woman in a lab coat, peering intently into a periscope looking for God knows what. Allied shipping, I suppose. It struck me then, and now, as I remember this delightful episode in my life, that not everyone could or would do this for a living. I remember thinking that doctors must be truly insane. Now I just realize that doctors and all the other professionals are simply different types of people. Doctors, lawyers, ministers, and, professional soldiers — the four traditional professions — require people who are willing to do some very bizarre, technically difficult, intellectually challenging, and emotionally draining, but absolutely necessary activities for the benefit of society and their fellow human beings.

Professionals go through extensive training that is almost cult-like in its intensity and focus. They spend years in intensive, almost brutal training, are constantly exposed to the intimidation of their instructors, superiors, and licensing boards, and, are handed almost from the outset, enormous and mind-numbing responsibilities. As a reward, we are paid better than the run of society. Most of us live in better neighborhoods and send our kids to better schools. Of course, as our careers progress, there are other rewards too. Broken marriages. Alcoholism. Drug abuse. Doubts. The pressure can be enormous, and the rules we play by, our various codes of ethics, are very different and artificial compared to the conventional ideas of such things entertained by the rest of society.

In this book, I propose to examine ethics in general, and, to apply the concepts and principles uncovered to the professions. To do this, I will start with a discussion of human beings. All of us, even lawyers, after all, are human beings. Certain things are possible for us and certain things are obviously beyond consideration. We are what we are because of our human nature. We need, accordingly, to discover what we are as human beings and how we are composed in order to understand what is possible for us ethically.

I would like to start this discussion on ethics and morality with a tale of the Montgomery County Ohio Democratic Party. You may well ask what the Democratic Party has to do with morality or ethics. Well, I have to start somewhere.

Montgomery County, Ohio, with its county seat at Dayton

is actually a history lesson. All of the stereotypes apply.
Republicans go to the country club. Democrats are drawn
from the labor unions and various ethnic minorities that live
in the city. The county is Republican; the city is Democratic.

The Chairman of the Democratic Party is an old-fash-
ioned political boss. He rose through the labor unions and
after a bloody revolution in the late '60s gained control of
the party. This gentleman has run the party unquestioned
and at his own whim for the last decade and a half. Of late,
the Chairman has taken to spending half of the year on his
boat in Florida. Nonetheless, by his visits to Dayton and by
close telephone contact, he has kept his finger on the pulse
of the city. Or at least no one would dare say otherwise.

During the summer of 1991 the Prosecutor of
Montgomery County Ohio, a Democrat, who had held his
office for 30 years and was a winner of seven general elections, announced his retirement. This, of course, was very
interesting to the Prosecutor himself since he found out
about his retirement through the newspapers. But, knowing
the Chairman and being the good Democrat that he had
been, growing up in the system as we all did, he did the only
reasonable thing and packed his fishing rods and golf clubs
and fell on his sword. The Prosecutor assumed, as did everyone else, that he would be succeeded by one of his senior
trial counsels, a man in his mid-forties and a phenomenally
successful trial attorney. In fact, this attorney was even
referred to as the "heir apparent."

The Chairman of the Democratic Party had different
ideas, however, and decided for God knows what reason —
and the Chairman needed no reason; he was omnipotent —
that a friend and crony of his, not the heir apparent, would
become the endorsed candidate of the Democratic party. In
the past this would be a virtual guarantee of election.
Further, the Prosecutor's Office with approximately seventy
politically-appointed attorneys was a rich source of funds
and manpower for upcoming elections, and was a prize for
anyone seeking political power in the county.

At any rate, negotiations ensued at the local party headquarters — a brick union-hall-looking building festooned

with ancient posters of John Kennedy and even F.D.R. (in fact, if I could ever steal that picture of Roosevelt for myself, I'd be a happy man). The Chairman was unmoveable. No one had ever dared question him in the past, and they weren't about to start it now.

The heir apparent, however, was by nature a person who loved to fight — he was a successful trial attorney after all — and he was independently wealthy, a sine qua non for American politics in the late twentieth century. Ain't democracy wonderful?

Peace talks broke down. The central committee, all followers of the Chairman, endorsed the crony. Big surprise. The heir apparent called in his closest friends in the Prosecutor's Office and decided to fight. After outlining the threats and difficulties of a rebel campaign, the heir, a popular guy previously, was left with four supporters. Nonetheless he pushed ahead and attempted to drum up support.

Threats, not idle threats, but very real threats, were made bluntly to the attorneys in the office, all political appointees as mentioned, that their jobs would be on-the-line if they supported the rebel cause.

I, good reader, like many others, was caught in the middle. I also, like many others, was not independently wealthy. I did not know the heir apparent very well. In the past four years that I had been in the office he could barely remember my name when we met by chance in the elevator. However, one of my closest friends was an enemy of the political crony slated to take over the office, and he'd be fired immediately if the crony was successful. Another friend was one of the four original supporters of the heir and would also be ruined. When I was approached early on by my friends, although I had been a life-long Democrat and would have cut my own hand off if it ever reached for the Republican lever in the voting booth, I joined the rebels out of personal loyalty. There was also the additional fact that the heir apparent was decidedly more qualified to take over the office, but in reality, loyalty was my motive. Again, democracy won.

The first overt act of rebellion was a voter registration

drive on the west side of Dayton. This was a stronghold of the Chairman and the old guard. Anyone who took part in this action would be destroyed professionally and financially if the Chairman's crony won. Twelve people showed up. Me among them. The drive was successful finding surprising support in enemy territory.

The fight carried on for seven months. At night, I discovered in later conversations with my friends, many of us sat up watching our sleeping mates and children wondering what we had done to them. As we encouraged more of our friends to support us, we shivered under the responsibility for them should things go wrong.

In the end, on June 2, 1992, the rebel forces won a decisive victory in the Ohio primary. The Chairman retreated to his boat in Florida. The crony's career was destroyed, and we all got very, very drunk.

Now, you may well ask why the concerns of a handful of political appointees in Dayton, Ohio, of all places, should be of interest to anyone. Frankly, the moral decisions of about twenty people, setting aside the lost jobs, firings, ruined careers, and severed marriages, had the most far-reaching of consequences.

In the fall of 1992 Bill Clinton needed to carry the midwestern states. The heart of this region and an electorally rich state was Ohio. In Ohio there are only two Democratic strongholds: Cleveland and Dayton. To win Ohio Clinton had to firmly take both areas. Cleveland was strong but Dayton, the scene of the recent civil war and a weakened Democratic machine, was in question. There was so much ill-feeling that a visit by Al Gore was necessary to enforce a truce. Of course, Clinton won Ohio which put him over the top in electoral votes. The truce had held and he readily carried Montgomery County, one of the only two counties he carried in Ohio, as predicted. I know. I was there that night also. Not at Democratic Headquarters, since none of us would set foot there, but at Clinton Headquarters a half a mile away.

In short, the moral decisions, the personal loyalties, and the weaknesses of a handful of people, potentially threatened to alter the course not only of the primary race for county prosecutor, but the course of the national presidential election, the course of history itself. Had the division in the party in this little Ohio county held, the Democrats would not have been able to take the State of Ohio.

I use this story about the Montgomery County Democratic party to illustrate a point about morality and ethics. As can be seen, ethics and morality are about conflict. They are about choosing from competing alternatives. It may be countered that one is presented with many choices in life, such as what flavor of ice cream to order, and that most of these choices have no moral content whatsoever. This is undeniably true. What then makes certain choices "moral" or "ethical" and others morally neutral? Probably the same reason that the philosopher Wittgenstein determined that some things are art and others are not. That is, because the artist, or in our context, the moral actor, says they are.

I don't mean to be flippant about this, but the subjectivity of morality is a fact. For instance, during the great grape boycott of the 1960s, a vast number of people were blissfully unaware that to buy table grapes was to support an evil dehumanizing system of farm labor. For them, the purchasing of a bunch of grapes was simply a culinary matter without any political or moral content. For those involved with or aware of the United Farm Workers Union, the decision to buy fruit was a gravely moral matter. Knowledge and belief were the key. (Why, I myself refused to purchase Honduran cigars during the days of the Contras since Honduras permitted the Contras to keep bases on their soil. Fortunately Panamanian cigars were better. Then that bum Noriega took away one of my few innocent pleasures — much to the delight of my family, friends, and anyone caught in enclosed quarters with me.)

The key to ethical behavior then seems to be the recognition of ethical problems. This recognition is dependent on knowledge. This knowledge leads to a preliminary labeling. Again, the problem, the conflict, is the essence of ethics. Without conflict there would be no awareness of good or evil. Knowledge, recognition, is necessary for ethics to exist and all knowledge is possible only when an object or situation is presented to consciousness. Nothing gains the attention of consciousness like opposition or conflict. Conflict generates the necessary emotional charge, strength or feeling to bring a situation above the level of consciousness and present it squarely to the conscious mind.[1]

This raises a further question for the thesis that ethics essentially involves conscious conflict. Is it not possible that some people are so well brought up and have received such thorough moral training that they habitually do the right thing without having to think about it at all? This necessarily raises the question whether morality can be unconscious. I was raised as a Roman Catholic. We were taught that children younger than seven years of age and insane people could not be held accountable for their actions since they were unable to know or recognize that what they did was right or wrong. One could argue, therefore, that if one group of people cannot be considered to act with any moral content simply because they do not recognize the moral implications of their actions, that anyone who fails to recognize these implications also cannot be considered to act morally. In other words, the little old church lady in the flowered dress is no more ethical or moral than the asylum inmate since her acts are equally devoid of recognition and awareness. They are unconscious, lacking in the conflict that brings recognition.

But it might be countered that the difference between the church lady and the insane person is not that they both do not recognize the moral conflict inherent in the situation, but rather that the one nonetheless is at least capable of recognizing competing moral forces while the other, due to mental or physical infirmity, is not. In other words, if the church lady thinks about it she can see the moral implications of the situation. Most times, due to her training, she does not. However, she is capable if she so desires. But that begs the question: To want to do something requires an exercise of will; a use of force or energy.

If the lady is not aware of a conflict herself, of course, she may have the situation presented to her by an outside act.

Sort of like a pop quiz. However, even in this academic situation, her interest has had to be drawn to a situation, information conveyed, and ultimately a problem recognized before judgment can be exercised. For this to happen two distinct positions or forces must be delineated and recognized. Again, therefore, opposition and conflict arise.

It may be premature in this discussion to speak of psychic energy, but what moral training seems to do is to displace the energy that would normally be produced by opposing moral imperatives by rechanneling the pathways (or "gradients" as Jung called it) of this psychic energy away from consciousness.[2] In other words, unexamined robot behavior occurs unconsciously — the church lady does not even consider reading Lady Chatterly's Lover — and any excess energy caused by the tension that the titillating interest of Lawrence's book may have produced will be drawn off and deposited in some other unconscious network of the mind to be used again in some other activity such as censoring books or burning witches. Psychic energy has to go somewhere. Suppression of conflict and the channeling of the attendant energy charge simply causes an abscess somewhere else.

In short then, since the habitual do-gooder, the church lady and insane persons, the psychopath, are equivalent in the mental assessment or lack thereof, of their behavior, they are all morally neutral; that is, they are incapable of moral or ethical action. Only those who consciously recognize opposing courses of behavior in a situation and who consciously label this conflict as "moral" can be said to be ethical or moral. Conscious moral awareness is a necessity and consciousness is only captured by those matters having a sufficient psychic energy charge to force themselves above the line of consciousness. Psychic energy is produced by tension and tension is generated by opposition — conflict.[3]

The idea of conflict as the dominant element for human affairs is not new. The applicability, however, is more often centered in politics and social philosophy. This is the case in the most prominent proponent of conflict theory, Thomas Hobbes.

Hobbes was a seventeenth century English philosopher who spent a great deal of his time in France. Probably not a bad idea. At any rate, Hobbes, in attempting to explain the existence of government and organized societies had recourse to a mythical "state of nature."[4]

This state of nature was the original condition of human beings. In this state Hobbes believed that it was every person for him or her self. Individuality, in the most extreme form possible, was the essence of the human being.[5]

Because of this human essence of greed and egocentricity, humankind was in a constant state of war.[6] Each person against every other. However, since this state of constant warfare was detrimental to an individual's comfort, and, since nothing else could be accomplished in a constant state of warfare, human beings surrendered some — actually as little as possible — of their individual freedom to a referee — the government.[7]

For Hobbes, the government was a necessary evil. Its primary function was security and very little else.[8] Additionally, the concept of good and evil was for Hobbes entirely relative; most nearly approaching the pleasure and pain responses of animals.[9] After the development of the state, good and evil were arbitrarily defined by the sovereign.[10]

Another such thinker in the West was Niccolo Machiavelli. Machiavelli, like Hobbes, believed in the fundamental egotism of human beings, and, also like Hobbes, opted for a firm central government as the only means of keeping human beings from destroying themselves and of allowing their more creative and cultural tendencies to develop.[11]

In the East, in China, this view led to the oppressive Legalist Regime of the Ch'in Dynasty. Again, strict, centralized political control was the solution for the constant state of war that had plagued China for centuries.[12]

Political theory, however, is not the same as ethics or morality. It may well be influenced by ethical or moral considerations, but as the cases of Machiavelli and Hobbes demonstrate, a political solution to conflict does not necessarily involve morality. Indeed, Hobbes makes that point in his concept of good and evil as relative in almost biological terms.[13] Machiavelli's name, of course, is infamous worldwide for his discounting of ethical and moral considerations.

The reason that a statist approach to conflict fails to involve morality is that as indicated, moral and ethical conflicts are by nature individual and internal. Like the church lady, one may be forced by an external agency, the State, to act "good." However, since there is no alternative choice possible, morality is not involved. And, using the model of the church lady, the withdrawal of energy from the primary, personal conflict, leads to its expression elsewhere; in mass destructive behavior such as in Nazi Germany and during the cultural revolution in China.[14]

Proponents of statism argue that the ends of their measures, that is, peace and security, are moral and, therefore, morality is involved, at least at the stage of the preliminary choice to pursue a statist policy. However, this is like the choice to get drunk. The goal is to feel happy, but once the choice is made, both consciousness and conflict disappear.

Ethics and morality therefore cannot be based on mass political commitments. Ethics is not politics. How then is the individual to face conflict, which is the basis of ethics and morality?

An intermediate position between that of statism (or for that matter any sort of institutionalized narcolepsy), and rudderless individualism, is that of the profession of arms itself. In the West this is called chivalry. In the East, *Bushido*.

Both chivalry and *Bushido* are terms denoting not only a profession, a soldier or cavalryman, but a code of conduct. Both reached their apogee at approximately the same time; between the tenth and twelfth centuries A.D. During this period both systems were concerned with actual warfare. Both chivalry and *Bushido*, were influenced and permeated by religion: Christianity in the West, and Buddhism, especially Zen Buddhism, in Japan. Indeed, the religious influence was so strong as to itself induce the wars of the Crusades.

The decline of both systems also occurred at the same time. In Japan, the *Shogunate* put an end to continual civil and feudal war;[15] in Europe, massed bowmen and gunpowder

made the armored knight obsolete.[16] In both areas the warrior code became refined and mixed with ethical and aesthetic considerations. Romance and courtly love — heavily
influenced by Christian ideals in Europe — became of great
interest to the unemployed soldiery.[17] Artificial combat,
jousts and duels, kept the armored part of the code alive. It
was also at this time that the process of combat as ritual and
art became apparent to both cultures. More will be said of
this admixture of art and arms below.

The reason for stating that the codes of the orders of
chivalry and of the samurai represent a plausible model for
ethical conduct is that conflict is the subject matter of the
warrior's profession. The warrior exists for conflict. Since
conflict is the basis of ethics, a profession that constantly
studies, prepares for, and engages in conflict would be the
most direct and appropriate model for ethics.

The soldier's involvement with morality is a weighty matter since death is always and every day a real possibility. No
other profession, except perhaps medicine, so constantly
contemplates death. Every decision, whether purely a matter of physical technique, or one involving loyalties or alle-
giances, is made in the shadow of death. Hence, the necessary admixture of religion and the Code.[18]

To overcome fear one must understand death. To understand death is to plan a strategy for meeting death. This
strategy comes from religion. While religion cannot address
all of the situations of the professional warrior, it can give
guidance and bounds to the inner strength of the knight or
samurai.

Now it might be countered that this is all well and good,
but very few people actively serve in an occupation that is
constantly involved with death. But we are all involved in the
profession of death. It is called human being. It is only that
most pursuits allow us to delude ourselves as to death's constant imminence. We have all heard and used the expression,
"I could be run over crossing the street." We all could. That
is precisely why a profession that brings our ultimate fate
clearly into focus should be our model, since by doing so,
delusion is kept to a minimum.

Further, conflict is a constant in life. While most of us don't get up in the morning and gird on chain mail and a morning star, as the story of the Montgomery County Prosecutor's race demonstrates, serious conflict and consequences can rear themselves in the most civil and middle class of occupations.

Certain occupations, and law comes immediately to mind, are more conflict-oriented than others. Life and death are not as common as in warfare, but life and death or other serious consequences are the outcomes of many, many trials.

Business is based on competition. Competition inevitably means conflict and confrontation between products, services, organizations, and people. Sales and marketing especially bring out situations of conflict.

Working within an organization or corporation also implies conflict. Our jobs are not guaranteed. We fight to hold them. We compete against each other. How many people in our modern corporate culture have been involved in power struggles, takeovers, and internal politicking? As with the prosecutors mentioned above, more often than we like, we must choose sides.

If we recognize the inherence of conflict in our lives, especially our professional lives, then it becomes more understandable that we take the standard for our behavior from those who have made a profession of conflict — the warriors.

It's been stated that the model for ethics in our competitive society should be the "Code" of the warrior; the samurai or the knight. However, "Code" is a misnomer. While all socicties propound intricately complicated rules of etiquette and law, these things being externally imposed and settled, "chipped in stone," are not the stuff of either ethics or morality. They can be the ossified products of ethics and morality. Ethics and morality, however, are the process of conflict.

If the "Codes" of *bushido* and chivalry are not a static set of rules, then what are they? What they most nearly approach are works of art.

What is art? As stated earlier art is darn near anything

removed from the daily "everyday stream of unconscious, or near-consciousness" and presented to consciousness in such a manner as to draw attention and energy to itself and for itself as art. This is a snooty way of saying that art is anything the artist presents to us and calls "art." This is the position finally arrived at by Wittgenstein in his long analysis of the subject. If one adds a feeling tone and the drawing of energy from everyday consciousness, it is very like the opinions of Schopenhauer,[19] who will be discussed below. Art is unpredictable. It is absorbing. It draws one out of the everyday, humdrum existence. Ethics is, by definition, almost the same. When a conflict occurs in one's life, one's attention is drawn. One is removed from one's everyday semi-conscious patterns of behavior. As with art, one must react in a way that stands out.

No two works of art are the same. That is the nature of art. Similarly, no two conflict situations requiring an ethical stance are the same. That is why, while rules and codes, like the rules of perspective and drawing, can help in the creation of a work of art, they are not the essence of ethics. Every ethical situation, like every work of art, is unique.

How then is one to practice ethics if there are no rules? Again, two points from the martial arts help to answer this question. The first is the concept of "virtue." Virtue does not mean some sort of milquetoasty, tee-totalling, prissy do-gooder. The original meaning of virtue was strength. Strength is something internal. Like physical strength, it can be developed, but is a reserve, a fluid, flexible structure; not a rigid ossified, dead skeleton.

The other applicable concept from the martial arts is that of *Budo*. While *bushido* refers to the classical warrior's way and contemplates nothing less than armed warfare, *Budo* refers to a more general "way of life." *Budo* is actually a form of spiritual training. It uses the forms, weapons, and training of the martial pursuits as a metaphor for the conflicts of the spirit and the conquest of life.[20] While *Budo* many times concentrates on artistic and aesthetically pleasing presentation, this artistic presentation is not the essence or goal of *Budo*, but is also simply part of the rigorous training of the spirit.[21] Years and years of rote training in physical forms and techniques are required before one can develop the spirit to the point where "it" acts and the everyday personality is overridden.[22] This "it" that acts, however, is not unconscious, but "superconscious" since it is like a sword that hacks away the dross that surrounds a situation and cuts to its uniqueness.

Now it may well be queried at this point as to how this spirit of highly trained *Budo* is different from that of a religiously well-trained church lady. The answer is that it depends upon what the church lady is exercising when she engages in moral behavior. If what she does is an unconscious act totally conditioned by externally applied "rules," then her behavior is simply that, behavior. Mindless, possibly blameless, but not ethical or moral actions which require conscious energy and opposition. If, on the other hand, her actions stem from a strong, that is "virtuous" spirit that acts decisively to achieve what is right in a given situation, not due to some unquestioned imperative, but due to its own intuitive strength, then the church lady and the *Budo* master would be one and the same.

That intuition and decisiveness are required for ethical action is demonstrated by the nature of situations requiring ethical action. Ethical dilemmas do not appear in well-stocked libraries over snifters of brandy and fine (albeit not Honduran) cigars when one has all the time in the world to leisurely pursue every nuance and then with a burrumph and an adjustment of one's tweeds, the answer springs forth as the only reasonable alternative. Ethical problems are more like this: A vicious and exceedingly violent drug dealer, whom the police have tried for years to get off the streets, and his gang attack a lower level drug dealer whose mathematical training has never progressed beyond the first grade level. The lower level guy owes money. The attack takes place in the middle of an intersection in a poor, residential area. The lower level guy is beaten, pistol-whipped, and robbed of money and a gold herringbone chain at gunpoint. Several teenage girls witness the attack from their porches nearby. The girls know the drug dealer, know his well-deserved reputation for violence, and experience it first-hand on this occasion. Further, the drug dealer knows them.

The police are called and the girls, before they can think, give full statements and are listed as witnesses. They are subpoenaed by the prosecutor, but due to constant telephone threats they refuse to come to the prosecutor's office.

In the interim, the low-level drug dealer, the guy that was beaten in this instance, begins to waffle on his testimony. This may have something to do with his receipt of $1,000 as condolence from his old friend the higher-level drug dealer. Some friendly detectives point out his compelling civil responsibility, and the low-level dealer makes the moral decision to keep the $1,000 and testify anyhow. Nonetheless, the low-level dealer disappears.

The week before trial, the low-level dealer calls the prosecutor and reiterates his intention to testify, but appears at no further pre-trial conferences.

The girls, meanwhile, continuing to get threats from the drug gang, are told by the prosecutor that police officers would bring them forcibly to court if they do not show up.

The day of the trial arrives. The victim, the low-level drug dealer has not appeared. Police officers are sent to search for him. A jury is picked in an effort to stall for time. Opening statements are made. The prosecutor can present his witnesses in any order. He could present the girls first and buy more time for the complainant to appear as he stated he would. If the prosecutor does so, he knows that these girls will be on their own after the trial. If the victim fails to appear, the high-level drug dealer will be back on the street. This, however, is the best chance the police have had in years to get this violent, psychopathic drug dealer put away for a long period of time. The alternative is to dismiss the case since time for a constitutional speedy trial has run and no further continuances can be granted. Further, since the jury has been picked, there can be no retrial for double-jeopardy reasons.

Does the prosecutor put the girls on and endanger their lives? Does he dismiss and let the drug dealer go free? What if the victim appears? There is no good answer. There is no one and only one answer that can reasonably be deduced for this situation. An instant decision must be made, however. This is where intuition and virtue are exercised. This is where spiritual and *Budo* training play their part. (For those who want to know, I dismissed the case. The lives of the girls were more important to me. I did not like it, and will get this guy eventually, but this was not the time. His release had to be borne with patience, strength, and resolve. Besides, I set him up for a federal parole revocation. Sometimes it's ethical to shoot someone in the back.)

In *Budo*, the three threads of ethics come together: conflict, art, and strength. As discussed, conscious conflict is required for ethical decisions to be possible. Unconscious or unquestioned activity is simply "behavior," not unlike that of the rats in a maze at some research laboratory. The opposition of two competing courses of action produce the energy necessary to raise the conflict to a level of consciousness. Artistic presentation is the manner in which the situation is presented to consciousness as out of the ordinary, and, strength, virtue, is developed by spiritual training that allows the artist, the ethical actor, to intuit and then actually create in the physical world, the ethical action that resolves the conflict. Martial arts training, especially *Budo* with its emphasis on spiritual training, is thus the ideal model for ethics.

At this point it should be recognized that our discussion of ethics and morality has been somewhat abstract. We have argued against a system of unquestioned and rigid external rules in favor of the internally generated idea of virtue or strength. What we must not do, however, is to make virtue itself into a "thing." Rules and codes easily lend themselves to this situation since they are complete and unchanging; "chipped in stone," so to speak. Virtue, like physical strength, however, depends on constant activity and practice. While abstract "rules" and laws can, theoretically, exist without human beings, there can be no virtue without a real human actor. One cannot meaningfully talk about strength without including the concept of who is exercising that strength. Ethics as the exercise of virtue requires, starts from, and ends with, the real human being.

The idea of the human being as central to philosophy is not new or unique. Immanuel Kant placed man at the center of philosophy in his "Copernican Revolution" in thought in the eighteenth century.[23] Kant argued that it is all well and good to speak of so-called "first principles"; external, over-riding laws that supposedly exist independent of man such as mathematics or logic or certain other principles of science and thought, but without a real human being, how could there be any knowledge of these laws or principles? How could their existence be known? Further, if these principles must be known to be verified, are they not dependent on the knower? And if they are dependent upon the knower, they are subject to the limits of the knower's mind and organs of perception. How can it be known if something is true or false if one does not understand the principles of the instrument, in this case the human mind and body, through which the search for truth is conducted?

Kant dedicated his most famous and influential work to the exploration of the principles of "pure reason"; that is, to the principles of human perception and thought. He mapped the limits of both perception and thought, and thereby determined what could be known by the limited instrument that was the human being. From this starting point he derived his principles of both art and ethics.[24]

Prior to Kant, David Hume, the ultimate British Empirical philosopher, also began from an analysis of human perception, both physical and mental.[25]

In the East, especially in China, the human being had always been the center of philosophical discussion.[26]

All of these philosophers represent the basic insight that morality and ethics cannot exist without a moral actor — a living human being. Again, following Kant, it would be meaningless to speak about "unknown" moral principles, and that is precisely what they would be if there would be no persons to know and embody them. I use the term "embody" since it is also meaningless to speak of ethics or moral principles if these principles are not put into action. Knowing but not acting is no more moral or ethical than acting badly. Further, it is absurd to talk of some sort of transcendental moral principles if there are no situations in the real world to which they apply. This raises an interesting question: If general moral principles cannot exist without the situations to which they apply, but, if in any of these situations we claim (as Plato would argue) that we already know what is right and what is wrong, that is, that there is only one right answer or correct way of behaving, what comes first, the principle or the situation to which it applies? The chicken or the egg? Perhaps neither. Perhaps they arise together. If that is the case, both are intimately involved with the human actor. He generates or secretes both the situation that raises a moral question and its answer! If, therefore, the human being creates both the moral situation and the applicable moral principle, then there must be something in the composition, the intrinsic make-up of a human being that necessitates morality. It is necessary, therefore, to understand what a human being is, so as to fully understand the genesis of morality and ethics. By doing so, we will see what is possible for people in our world and what limitations there are for our actions. This will make our later discussions of virtue and the warrior codes more intelligible.

Originally in the West, the human being was seen as totally material. This being had a soul, as the Greek and Egyptian religions taught, but to the Milesian Greeks, this soul was also material, if made up of more subtle particles. The physical theory used to explain all of this was that of "Atomism." The basis of this theory was that the world, including humans, were composed of little material ball-bearings and space, or the void. The differing motions and groupings of these atoms made all of the different things seen in the world, including rocks, animals, people, and their souls.[27]

Unfortunately, the Atomists failed to explain what caused the motions of the atoms, and, why atoms, originally falling in straight lines through the universe like some sort of cosmic rain, would be attracted and grouped or clumped together in specific and stable ways. Since the atoms were all alike, how could qualities such as differing colors, shapes, sounds, textures, et cetera, arise? Further, how could human endeavors such as art, ethics, and religion be explained? A purely material approach cannot answer these questions. Indeed, modern physics itself would move away from such a crude materialism.[28]

Since the limitations of a purely materialistic view of both human beings and nature became increasingly apparent, the Athenian philosophers, Socrates, Plato, and Aristotle moved in another direction.

The Athenians were concerned primarily with ethics.[29] What was the correct and most pleasing way for a person to act? What constitutes good government and the good life? In order to answer these questions Plato proposed to examine the state by analogy with the faculties of the human being.[30]

For Plato, the human being was composed of a soul and a body. This soul was separable from the body in which it was imprisoned. Being stuck in matter, the faculties of the soul were blunted. The soul and the mind were forced to receive their information from the senses which only picked up the grossest of physical manifestations and which were consequently, subject to error.[31]

There was, however, another source of information for the soul. The mind could be used to rise above the body and the confusion of material existence and, in intellectual contemplation, view the transcendent intellectual "forms." These forms were the true essences of all things. They existed before the individual thing and the individual thing was what it was because it participated in its form.[32] An example would be a table. We instantly know whether a certain object is a table. We recognize it as such. It doesn't matter whether it has four, three, two, or one leg; it is a table. It could be broken and have legs missing; it is recognized as a table. It could be made of metal, wood, plastic; it is recognized as a table. It could be flipped over and floated on the river like a raft; it is still a table. How does one know a certain object is a table? According to Plato, because a part of our mind constantly views the eternal forms and thus compares the objects of the world with their transcendental essence.[33]

I use the word "transcendental" since these forms are the pure essences, and as such cannot be sullied by being mixed with matter.[34]

Plato, however, does not stop with material objects. More importantly, he asserts that there are forms of abstract entities such as justice, beauty, and the Good.[35] Plato also asserts that we already know the forms of these things since we viewed them before our birth when we were all disembodied souls. It is only through our descent into mentally dulling matter at birth that we "forget" the true nature of things. Education for Plato was thus a guided "remembrance" of things already innate in the human mind.[36]

This brings us to another point concerning the nature of human beings. For Plato, the soul is able to separate from the body, and, indeed, this is its natural state. The admixture with matter is unnatural and the human being is most truly himself or herself when separated from matter.[37]

Plato, however, goes further in his discussion of the soul. He divides it into three parts: The lower or vegetative soul which seeks nourishment, reproduction, and survival; the passionate soul which is the seat of the emotions; and, the intellect which views the Forms and acts rationally. Plato recognizes that all parts of the mind are necessary, but argues that the rational part should lead the others.[38]

The main problem with Plato's theory is that the Forms themselves are totally removed from the world. Since they are completely transcendent it is never explained just how they affect and shape the things of the world. Further, Plato stands at the beginning of the Western split between mind and matter.

Plato's student, Aristotle, rejected the transcendence of the Forms. Instead, Aristotle placed the Forms in matter and declared that all of the things in the world were composite; being made up of both matter and form. Matter makes the thing possible, while the form makes it what it is.[39] For the human being, if the soul is separated from the body, the resulting entity, therefore, cannot be human.[40]

Aristotle accepted Plato's three-part division of the mind, but pushed the analysis further stating that while human beings share the lower two parts of the mind with plants and animals, it is the rational part of the mind that makes a being human.[41] Aristotle also recognized that there is a part of the mind that is somehow eternal. As such it is, at least theoretically, capable of separating from the body. However, as stated above, whatever separates from the body cannot be human.[42]

The work on human beings did not progress much beyond the initial positions of Plato and Aristotle throughout the remainder of the ancient world. After the fall of Rome, the works of Aristotle were lost until the twelfth century. Consequently, the Platonic view of man dominated in the West. This was aided by the triumph of Christianity, which found Plato's disparagement of this world and his position concerning the existence of a separable soul quite congenial.[43] Unfortunately, Christianity was also a revealed religion and, as part of its dogma, believed in the "resurrection of the body."[44] This was not at all Platonic.

This tension between Platonism and Christian dogma remained until the rediscovery of the works of Aristotle in Arabic translation during the twelfth century. Aristotle's composite being again allowed Christians to incorporate the body into the human being. It made the resurrection of the body possible.[45] Unfortunately, Aristotle's old problem arose under a different guise. Christian dogma states that the total human being will reunite and rise again on Judgment Day. Yet during the period from death until Judgment Day, the body decays and the soul separates. So just what type of being do we have? It can't be human since the human being by definition is a composite of soul and body. In other words, human beings under this view go from human to non-human to human again! The tension of this position remained with the Christian West for the remainder of the Medieval period.

At the beginning of the Modern Era, René Descartes proposed to begin from the beginning again by doubting everything except those propositions presenting themselves as "clear and distinct" ideas. Descartes was a mathematician and physicist and derived his model of knowledge from the axiomatic method of geometry.[46]

Descartes asserted that he could doubt everything but

his own existence. In order to doubt he had to think; to think he had to exist. Descartes is, of course, remembered for the expression "I think, therefore, I am."[47]

Following his criteria of clear and distinct ideas, Descartes posited two substances: mind and matter. These are distinct substances since the idea of one does not involve the idea of the other. Mind involves thinking and no extension; matter, extension and no thought. Therefore, the human being is obviously composed of these two substances. Descartes claimed that the two are somehow joined together, but readily admitted that he could not adequately explain the connection.[48]

Descartes is also consistent in his application of his principles to the non-human. To Descartes, angels, unlike human beings, possess only one substance, that of mind. Animals, on the other hand, are purely material beings no better than cleverly constructed machines.[49]

René Descartes did not create the mind/body split that has plagued the West throughout its history, but he did present it in such clear relief that it has been unavoidable in the modern era. All philosophers and scientists after Descartes have had to address this problem — especially in relation to the nature of human beings

By using the model of mathematics as the basis of his philosophy, Descartes drew some interesting deductions concerning the human mind. Like Plato, who was also influenced by mathematics, Descartes believed that there could be no other way for a human being to think logically and deal with abstract principles unless the basic structures of these principles were already present in the human mind.[50] Note, unlike Plato, that Descartes placed these abstract principles in the human mind itself. They are placed there by God, but they are part and parcel of being human.[51] Descartes termed these rational structures of the human mind "innate ideas."[52] The philosophy of Descartes, based as it was on a mathematical model and the concept of innate ideas, was dubbed Rationalism.

On the other side of the Channel, English philosophers chose a different approach, beginning from sense perception. To these philosophers, all knowledge comes from the senses. The human mind, unlike that conceived of by Descartes, is originally blank. Experience fills this mind, which is active only in abstracting principles from the comparison of sense data.[53]

Concerning substance, the first British Empiricist, John Locke, accepted the two substances proposed by Descartes, but declared them to be merely useful abstractions after the actual fact of sense perception.[54]

Following Locke, Bishop George Berkeley declared that there only one substance — ideas.[55] Berkeley argued that if "to be" is "to be perceived," matter, an abstraction, is never actually perceived, only inferred. Therefore, it cannot exist. Ideas, however, are directly experienced. Accordingly, there is only one substance — mind.[56]

The final classical British Empiricist, David Hume, took Berkeley even further and asserted that the existence of the human mind cannot be proven because like matter, since all we perceive is individual ideas, there is no entity called "mind," only individual ideas. In fact, the concept of a "mind" itself is merely one more idea or mental perception in the flow of perceptions. What we call a human being is, therefore, merely a collection of perceptions that are associated by habit and erroneously united under yet another idea called "mind."[57] This view of man is astonishingly close to the Buddhist concept of skandas, or heaps of perceptions. The Buddhists also deny the existence of any organizing Self beyond these heaps of perceptions.[58]

Hume's analysis was devastatingly effective, so much so that Immanual Kant, the greatest Western philosopher since Thomas Aquinas, spent his life trying to reconcile the positions of the Rationalists and the British Empiricists.

Kant argued that while all knowledge is dependent upon and initiated by sense data, the human mind is not simply a blank slate, but has certain innate structures, not ideas, but structures that actively organize and shape the incoming sense data. These structures are the various categories of knowledge; quantity, quality, etc., and the transcendental "intuitions" of space and time.[59] Knowledge to Kant was the interaction of the innate structures of the mind and sense data.[60] The question as to whether these actually are two substances, and, indeed, if there is even an external world, is left unanswered.

Also of interest in Kant's work is the concept of the Ding-an-Sich, the "Thing-in-itself." Like Berkeley and Hume, Kant states that when we look at the things of the world, all we really experience are "qualities," for example, color, texture, shape, etc. Like Plato, however, Kant accepts the fact that the organization of these qualities or "bundles of perceptions", to use Hume's term, is not simply by chance, but due to some sort of organizing principle behind the perceptions. Unfortunately, however, this principle cannot itself be perceived, but has to be inferred. This principle is the thing-in-itself which must exist, but can never be proven to do so.[61]

G.W.F. Hegel extended Kant's insight into the active nature of the human mind. The centerpiece of Hegel's thought was the dialectic which consisted of three terms, a thesis or a proposition that is presented, an antithesis, or contrary or opposing proposition, and, the synthesis, or higher resolution of the conflict.[62] Unlike the symbolic logic of Aristotle in which contradictory or contrary propositions simply neutralize each other, in Hegel's schema, the contraries are "synthesized" and a solution containing elements of both, but not simply restricted to the lower propositions, is achieved. This synthesis then becomes a new thesis, etc.[63]

Nowhere is this model more important for Hegel than in its application to being, and specifically human being.[64] The human mind, according to Hegel, works on the principle of the dialectic. The thesis is the human with his or her internal innate mental structures, á la Kant and Descartes. The antithesis is the mind reaching out to the external world in perception since again, like Kant, Hegel makes the mind an active participant in perception. The synthesis consists of the mind bringing the data of perception back for itself, thereby giving meaning and value to the world.

The process is one of creation. The mind associates and combines sense data as with Locke, Berkeley, and Hume. It organizes and categorizes this data as with Kant, then, and this is the great insight of Hegel, it, the human mind, creates from this information. It creates science, art, religion, society, and culture — and ethics.

The human thus becomes the human the Creator. It is human nature to create a world. Animals may perceive. Even amoebas respond to sense stimuli. Higher animals have instincts and mental structures that may organize sense input and respond; but only humans create. Only humans can synthesize; that is, only humans can take the given of sense data and basic mental structures and add to them. The nature of human beings is creative activity.

Because of his emphasis on creativity, Hegel asserts that humans are continually creating their world. There is very little given and almost all things can be creatively changed. Hegel places great emphasis on history which he sees as the unfolding of human potential and artistry through time. The goal of human being and of history is to create more and more freedom and opportunities for self-expression.

Hegel's thought lies at the beginning of the nineteenth century. During the ensuing century, the physical sciences were to become more and more restrictive and materialistic. Hegel's philosophy of human creativity and artistic freedom opened broad vistas for Western cultures. Even those who criticized Hegel's thought paid tribute by arguing in Hegel's terms, that is, in terms of freedom and the contemplation of art.

One of Hegel's earliest critics, Arthur Schopenhauer, agreed that human beings create a world for themselves, but argued that the basis of this world was not reason, but a blind, instinctual will to exist.[65] The mind is only used by the will as a tool for survival. The center of activity thus lies somewhere below the conscious rational mind. As one can readily see, Schopenhauer's thought was to be a great influence on the later depth psychologists such as Freud and especially, Carl Jung, whose theories depend so much upon an instinctual, unconscious part of the mind.

For Schopenhauer, the goal of the enlightened person was to escape the demands of the will and find peace. One way to do this according to Schopenhauer was in the disinterested contemplation of art. Again, as with Hegel, art takes the principle place in his view of the human being.

Soren Kierkegaard was also critical of Hegel since, while again accepting the view that humans creates their own world, because humans, by nature are finite, that is, limited in time, his world is necessarily incomplete. Further, since both the world and its creator are incomplete, knowledge is not really possible. Because of this, the human, according to Kierkegaard, is human due to hisor her ability to doubt. This, of course, is similar to the starting point of Descartes.

However, Kierkegaard extends Descartes' insight by separating the human being from "things." Things are discrete entities. Since they are discrete objects, they are necessarily, at any one moment, complete. Since humans are by nature incomplete, they can never be a thing for themselves. To make a human a thing, as some forms of social science attempt, is to do violence to basic human nature.

Using Hume's analysis of mind as the collection of discrete "thought things," Kierkegaard further argues that the human being cannot be his or her thoughts. The human being is accordingly, beyond reason and therefore, a free actor.

Since the human actor is beyond reason, he or she acts on his or her beliefs and faith.[66] Kierkegaard's radical Christianity thus influenced his view of human beings.

While both Schopenhauer and Kierkegaard were self-avowed critics of Hegel, both also agreed with the view of the human as the creator of his world and an actor. Life becomes a work of art. Where these thinkers diverge from Hegel is in their emphasis on the irrational in human nature. This conflict between the rational and the irrational emphasis in human nature was played out until the end of the century.

Following Hegel, Karl Marx defined the nature of the human being as that of production. The human must create. However, social conditions affect the manner of this creation. Specifically, for Marx, the economic system current at his time, capitalism, made the commodities created more important than their human creators. In other words, the inhuman "thing" reduces the freedom of the human being; reduces the person.

Marx argued, beginning from Hegel's work, that humans must again take charge of their creations and make the "things" of his or her world more human and thus make that world more rational. He or she must heal the split between the thing and the person created by the imposed socio-economic system.

Friederich Nietzsche followed Schopenhauer's basic premises, but, unlike Schopenhauer, asserted that the irrational human will should be given free reign. To Nietzsche this will is the basis of human creativity. Like Schopenhauer, Nietzsche emphasized artistic creation, but to Nietzsche the sources of creation comes from the pressure of the will which forces the human to attempt an escape through either dreams or intoxication. Art is produced from these two sources. Dreams are the sources of the plastic arts. Music is produced from intoxication. Reason is irrelevant to the pressure to create.

Giving free reign to the will encourages a situation in which the will demands more and more from the world that it is creating. However, the will not only creates a surrounding world, but itself. As it demands more of the world, it demands more of itself, therefore the human being continually surpasses him or her self. Nietzsche demands that humanity recognize this and consciously create a better and grander human being; the Superman.[67]

Science during the nineteenth century also moved first to materialism and then to more evolutionary and more abstract and indeterminate methods. Darwin theorized that animal species were continually changing form and behavior in response to their environment. In physics, due to the discoveries on both the universal and atomic levels, mathematics and probability became more and more important. Matter was found to behave in indeterminate and only probabilistic manners. Light was seen as behaving both as a particle and as a wave.

Social scientists, however, attempted to stay with the old empirical and materialistic positions of the classical physics of the eighteenth century. The behaviorists, J.B. Watson and later B.F. Skinner, stated that internal states were irrelevant in any scientific study of human beings.[68] Only public, observable behavior is important. Further, human behavior can be explained as a simple stimulus/response pattern.[69]
Opposition to these philosophers came from modern biological Rationalists such as Konrad Lorenz, Stuart Hampshire, and Noam Chomsky. These philosophers argued that the human being is composed of certain innate biological structures and pre-programmed patterns of behavior. That these patterns are innate and not naturally learned is proven by the fact that species do fail to adapt. Dinosaurs died out when they failed to adapt their behavior to their new environment. If behaviorism were correct, species would change their behavior in response to new stimuli.

Further, these thinkers also point out that only certain types of behavior are evidenced by specific species; that there, therefore, seems to be a limit to the types of behavior possible. These limits, it is argued, are due to innate biological and genetic structures.

As the study of human behavior progressed, and as physical science became the model for philosophy in Britain and America during the twentieth century, and as political totalitarianism became pervasive, the positions of the irrationalist philosophers were raised to emphasize human freedom and indefinability.

Starting from the fact that a human being is not a complete "thing," the twentieth century irrationalists added a time dimension to human being. Science necessarily deals with "things." This is so because science must be able to limit its objects of study so as to exert experimental control. Because these things are complete, finished, they must necessarily exist in the past dimension. They can never change.

In contrast, since human beings are incomplete, they exist in the present and future dimensions.[70] Further, while a human being may be objectified, such a being can act contrary to its own interest, out of love for instance, and therefore, is independent of the past. Such behavior is, therefore, unpredictable. This unpredictability is the basis of human freedom and, accordingly, of human being itself. Finally, the human being has the ability to transcend him or herself. Martin Heidegger defined the human being as the only being who can question its own being; who can ask "Why do I exist?"[71] His successor, Jean Paul Sartre, followed with the observation that the human being has the power of negativity, that is, he or she has the power to say "no" to things as they are.[72] The human being is never satisfied. He or she always wants more. Therefore, he exercises his freedom by saying "no" to whatever is in favor of what could be.

The way this being exists, however, requires a "world." The human being is a mystery existing alongside the world, but he or she is inconceivable without choice as presented by a world. The human is truly a "worlded spirit" as stated by Karl Rahner.[73] The way this human expresses him or herself in this world is through the "body."

The human body, however, has a special status. It is not just another thing among things, which is the basic mistake of Plato, Descartes, and all the other dualistic philosophers. Nor is it a mere bundle of things as per Hume, Berkeley and the other empiricists. Instead, the body is a "quasi-object."[74] The key to understanding this position is the distinction between "have" and "is" presented by Steven Strasser.[75]

What I "have," I can get rid of. My toaster, my car, my books, I can give away and exist without. What I am, however, I cannot give away without ceasing to exist. Obviously, I cannot get rid of my body as I can my toaster. If I get rid of my body I cease to exist as a human being.[76] Further, my body, unlike other objects, is always assumed. I don't constantly carry my toaster around with me. I don't make all decisions with an unstated consideration for the preservation of my toaster — but I do for my body. My body is the way I exist in the world. It is the way I express my subjectivity in an objective world.[77] It is a continual work of art. Martial artists, dancers, and athletes have this insight to varying degrees.

The human being in the West, then, is a composite of a

mystery, a continuing field of expression — its body — and, a "world." While the body can be treated as an object, it can be so only temporarily. It has innate structures that shape its world, but, it has the freedom to transcend and ignore these structures and behave unpredictably and irrationally. The human being is a free, creative actor who expresses him or herself in a world of his or her own creation; acceptance being at least a minimal form of creation.

The importance of all this is that while the human being is a free, creative actor, he or she is also to a certain extent a public thing, a bundle of perceptions, and an irrational mystery transcending and negating the world. Where the emphasis lies depends upon where the actor places it or lets it be placed. It makes a great deal of difference ethically whether we are dealing with a totally determinable thing, a being whose actions are limited by genetics and innate mental structures, or, a totally free and undetermined being. If we are dealing with a totally determinable thing, there can be no ethics because there is no personal choice. If we are dealing with a delimited being, there can only be a restricted area in which ethical decisions are possible. Further, in such a being it is questionable whether bad decisions are unethical or based on ignorance or just stupid. It is only if the human being is seen as somehow undetermined and somehow beyond the world, that choices, and especially ethical choices, are possible. The possibility of making ethical choices implies the possibility of making choices against one's own interests. It implies irrationality.

But if one acts irrationally, doesn't one necessarily act without cues? If a person acts rationally, he or she will try to act in his or her own interest, or at the very least to preserve that interest. They will accordingly look to cues from their environment and then make a decision. Acting irrationally, however, one necessarily disregards the cues provided by the environment. How then does one know how to act? Without knowledge how does one decide how to act?

We seem to have arrived at the area of the Zen *Koan,* where we are forced to act by superseding all thought. Again, is this not the world of the Zen warrior? We shall see that it is in the chapters that follow. In the West, following Sartre, Camus and others, this type of action would be termed "absurd." Since we have mentioned Zen, perhaps we should look into the nature of the human as developed in the East, to determine if we arrive at the same conclusion from another perspective.

Unlike the West, whose intellectual orientation is based almost entirely on Greek models, the East has two basic cultural sources: India and China. This is not to say that these two giant cultures didn't influence each other, but the vast distances involved and the natural obstacles between them allowed each society to develop to a fairly advanced state without interference from the other. Further, the antiquity of each predates history.

Indian thought is an amalgam of the invading Aryans from the Steppes of Central Asia and the settled, darker Dravidian people. Aryan culture, as I have stated elsewhere[78] was Shamanistic. It placed value on poetic, prophetic visions, and on heroism in battle. The Dravidians, on the other hand, possessed a more settled Yogic culture.[79] The joining of these two aspects gave rise to a "magically" oriented system of thought in the sense of the manipulation of symbols and power through discipline and mind-control.[80]

The basis of Indian thought and society are the *Vedas*. There are four *Vedas*: the *Rg, Yajur, Sama,* and *Artharva*. The *Yajur* and *Sama Vedas* are books of mantras, and the *Artharva Veda* is a book of magical and ritualistic practices.[81] The *Rg* is the oldest and is believed to have been with the Aryans before their entry into India.[82]

There are six orthodox "schools" of Indian philosophy. These schools are termed "orthodox" since all six accept the authority of the *Vedas* and claim to be derived from them. In fact, the derivation of the schools is even further refined since in principle all six are claimed to be located in the *Upanishads* or, the secret, distilled teachings of the *Vedas*.[83]

While Westerners tend to view India as some sort of dreamy, psychic Disneyland, in fact, the *Vedic* sages were extremely practical and "humanistic." I use the term "humanistic" in an expanded sense since the Hindu teachers did not define the human being as simply a fleshy, pleasure-seeking lab rat, which is the association that we sometimes get in the West, but as a total being operating on many different levels. The *Vedas* are directed to all levels of the human being.

On the practical side, the *Vedas* establish the four stages of life, the four castes, the four values, and the four sciences.[84]

The four stages of life correspond to the four aspects of the *Vedic* literature and four types of study, since to the Hindu thinkers life is for learning so that seeing the truth, one may become it. Realization, which sets one free from ignorance, error, and pain is the goal of life.[85] The four stages of life are the student phase, where one is free of responsibilities and has the time for simple rote memorization; the householders phase, where one has the responsibilities of career and family and little time for more than the formalities of the application of one's knowledge, but where one does learn about life; the stage of retirement, where one is still involved with one's mate, the other duties of life having been diminished, permitting reflection and concentration; and, finally, the stage of renunciation, represented by the Upanishads, where one is given the higher principles and ceases to make new karma, preparatory for attaining release.

The four castes are the *sudras*, or man-in-the-street whose material duties and lack of sophistication permit him only a share in unconscious mass religious expression; the *vaishya* or merchant caste, which has a bit more time and inclination to attend to religious duties and philosophical exploration; the *kshatriyas*, or warrior caste, which lives by and has an understanding of practical abstract principles such as loyalty, honor, and courage, and which has the discipline and leisure to begin serious philosophical study; and, finally, the *Brahmans,* who through past service and effort have been rewarded in this life with the leisure and intellect to pursue philosophical study exclusively.[86]

Concerning the caste system, it is believed that one is born into one's particular place in society due to one's own choice and effort in past lives.[87] This belief in reincarnation makes the caste system an expression of the learning principle behind Indian thought and removes it from the realm of a capricious and cruel joke. Three basic beliefs are agreed upon by the orthodox schools: First, as mentioned, the world is a means to knowledge; second, physical existence is the result of karma or the results of past actions and certain latent tendencies (*samskaras*); third, that there is an eternal, non-dualistic Self and that finding that self is the goal of life.[88]

According to Indian thought, participation in the world is necessary to the finding of the self. One cannot transcend life if one has not lived. One cannot learn without going to school. Accordingly, the four stages of life and the four castes are practical acknowledgements of the real situations in which human beings find themselves, and a recognition of the different limits and opportunities the various aspects of real life present for one's continuing religious education.

A further recognition of real human life is evidenced by the four values: Wealth, pleasure, duty, and salvation. This is not a hierarchy. No one value is exalted above the others. Instead, all are recognized as involved in each other.[89]

Wealth is pursued so that one can have pleasure. Pleasure reminds one of one's duties to the world that provides such pleasures. Duty leads to a desire for and appreciation of release and salvation. Salvation is pleasure and wealth.[90]

The four sciences are linked with the four values, and are the sciences of the wealth of things, pleasure, responsibility and position, and, release and salvation.[91]

Indian philosophy is, therefore, not some bloodless, ascetic, otherworldly illusion, but is firmly based in the real life of real, concrete human beings, recognizing and incorporating such things as the accumulation of money and property, and such pleasures as sex, food, music, and art.

This is a very different approach to human beings from that of the West. In the West, man seems to have been dissected away from the everyday environment. There is thus a continuity in method from the abstract analysis of philosophical principles of the Greeks to that of "controlled experiments" of modern scientists; be they physical or social. In other words, to find out what a human really is we must remove him or her from concrete life and place him or her in a totally artificial setting — created we must truthfully observe — by the experimenter just as with any other abstract work of art — and having thus limited him or her, say, domine, domine, domine, this is the real human essence.

But how can this type of artificial limitation be justified as accurate? It is like putting a tiger in a small box which will drive him mad and then saying that it is an intrinsic nature of all such tigers to be mad.

Instead, the Indian — and Chinese thinkers, for that matter — try to include as much of human life in the human being as possible.

This principle applies not only to the physical and social world as included in the concept human being, but also to the subtle world. The Self that is to be sought is also included in the world. It can be immediately felt and known and is very much like Descartes' starting point except that it is not simply defined by thinking.

The Indian philosophers are very careful to distinguish the self from substances or "things," such as perceptions or mental images. The Self, *atman,* is never-changing, and is, therefore, always a subject never an object — very similar to the "person" of the religious existentialist.[92] Like the person, the self or atman is continually more than itself. In Hinduism, this concept leads to the identification of atman, the immanent, but unlimited self, with *Brahman*, or the transcendent self.[93] *Atman* and *Brahman* are therefore, one, and are both in and beyond or alongside of the world. Like the human body, they are inescapable and always assumed. In order, therefore, to understand human being, it is necessary to understand the self which is so integrally involved with and in the world.

The *Vedic* sages recognized four subcategories of self, or, four "selves." Each was correlated with a type of human consciousness since, like Kant, these thinkers realized that only that which comes through the human mind can be known, and it can only be known in the final form in which consciousness presents it to itself.[94] The four selves are accordingly; the bodily self, which is associated with the working

▶▶

state; the empirical self, or "bundle of perceptions," associated with the dream state; the self in the dreamless sleep, which exists only in abstraction after the fact like the *Ding-an-Sich* of Kant and Schopenhauer; and, the absolute self, which exists in pure inwardness, that is, pure consciousness without any admixture.[95] While the bodily and empirical selves are objects among objects, and the deep-sleep self is object for others, and an isolated subject, the absolute self is neither subject nor object. In that sense it goes beyond the "pure subject" of the existentialists.

Following the four sciences, the *Vedic* thinkers define the selves in terms of pleasure, that is, in terms of what types of objects they enjoy. The bodily self enjoys gross objects; the dream self, subtle objects; the deep-sleep self, no objects (but only because of ignorance) and, finally, the absolute self, no objects because it is beyond subject and object.[96]

Again, the self is beyond subject and object, but it is on a continuum beginning in this world. Its overflow is, therefore, something that cannot be separated from the world. How is this possible?

To answer, one must understand the concept of the five sheaths or *kosas*, and the idea of *prana* or life-energy.

The Self is conceptually seen in its individual aspect as the atman. In its transcendental aspect it is called Brahman. *Brahman* and *atman* are actually one and the same. *Brahman* is derived from the root word brh, meaning to grow or evolve.[97] As such, it has biological connotations that relate it to virute which has a similar basis, as will be seen. It is, therefore, derived from a verb, and as such indicates action or a process.

Brahman evolves or grows through the five sheaths or kosas. The five sheaths are matter, life, mind or perceptual consciousness, self-conscious reason, and non-dual bliss.[98] The first three of these sheaths would be the areas of study included in both Western Rationalism and Empiricism. The fourth, self-conscious reason, is very much like the Absolute of Hegel. The last, non-dual bliss, perhaps is the field of the religious mystics. It is to be remembered, however, that these sheaths are objective cloaks or skins that the

▶▶

atman-Brahman assumes, but like a mask, are not *Brahman* themselves.

Since *atman*, the individual and *Brahman*, the universal, are the same, the human also possesses and evolves through the five sheaths. Further, because of the identity of *atman* and *Brahman*, the innermost nature of the human is god.[99] The human being is therefore, the meeting place, the habitat, the field of enjoyment of the gods.[100] His or her organs and processes are ruled and directed by the gods. The gods, however, are only aspects of *Brahman*, and are, therefore, subordinate to the human being.[101]

This continuum of *Brahman* or the self through the five sheaths precludes any rigid division or dissociation between mind, matter, and spirit such as is found in the West. Indeed, the ideas of "physical" or "mental" are almost meaningless in Indian thought since all levels interpenetrate each other.

Since the human mirrors the universe, the laws that compose the human being and the universe are one and the same. And since there is no division between mental and physical actions, actions in one area of the continuum reverberate throughout the whole. This is the basis of the yogic philosophy, one of the six orthodox schools of Hinduism.

The goal of Hinduism as stated, is release from the attachments of the world and a return to the universal self. In order to do this, yogic practice consists of withdrawing energy from the senses and thereby, from the world. The mind itself, also considered a sense organ, is also deprived of energy.

The physical postures and meditation techniques of yoga are used to calm both mind and body. If these elements are calmed, they are using the bare minimum of energy. The remaining energy is thus concentrated and then expanded so as to make the final identification of the *atman* with the universal *Brahman*. Yogins use the image of a pond to exemplify this point. If the water is disturbed, one cannot see clearly into the depths. However, when the surface is calm and all impurities are removed, the bottom can clearly be seen. Thus, ignorance is dispelled by the calming of the mind and body and the Yogin can clearly see his or her true nature as one with *Brahman.*[102]

Again, since the human being is essentially identical to the universe, the human being can make use of universal principles, principles of "physics" in the Greek sense, as nature, in order to effectuate his or her goal of universal consciousness. One of these principles is *prana* or the life energy that permeates the cosmos. By drawing in and controlling this universal energy, the human being can gently activate and alter the balance of elements, or *gunas,* that compose the human body.[103] *Pranayama,* or the practice of breath control, specifically rhythmic breathing, therefore, implies some sort of rhythm to the energy of the universe. As we shall see below, the laws of energy are intimately bound with virtue and ethics.

Taking this a step further is another of the classical schools of Indian thought, the *Mimansans.* The *Mimansans* place great emphasis on the *Vedas*, the revealed books of the Hindus. However, this emphasis is not merely on the content of these books, but on the rhythm of the sounds, the musical arrangement of the syllables themselves which compose the *Vedic* writings.[104] Very much like the Pythagoreans of the West, the *Mimansans* believe that the universe is actually and ultimately composed and created by vibrations.[105] The music of the spheres so to speak. To the *Mimansans,* the *Vedic* hymns and poetry mimic and contain within their rhythms the key to the cosmic vibrations.[106] Accordingly, the *Mimansans* developed a science of vibrations. To the *Mimansans*, the rituals performed in accordance with the *Vedic* books are not merely some sort of appeasement of the gods, but an actual scientific manipulation of the vibrations of the cosmos, and thereby of the cosmos, the universe, itself.[107] All things, even the gods are actually only "sound bodies," vibrational patterns — which can be changed, diminished, or amplified.[108]

Ethically then, the *Mimansans* and, in all probability, the Yogic practitioners, would understand action or karma, to use the Hindu word, in vibrational terms. Using the pond analogy again, if one acts and disturbs the water, ripples fan out in all directions. They may overlap with other ripples or karma and a new frequency or pattern would be created. This process continues until all of the energy in the pond is dissipated. The actor thus may be responsible not only for the initial act, but all succeeding results. These results are themselves both the punishment and reward for the act. The *Mimansans*, therefore, attempt through specific actions, that is *Vedic* rituals, to control the frequencies created. The Yogins attempt to draw off the energy.

The involvement of the concept of energy in this discussion of ethics necessarily brings us to the threshold of Chinese thought. As I have stated in my previous book *The Tao of Bioenergetics*, China is a society based on energetics. The ultimate root of Chinese philosophy, science, religion, and art in the concept of a universal, all-pervasive energy called *Qi. Qi* composes the heavens, the earth, and the human being, wherein the energies of heaven and earth are joined and mixed. Chinese stellar astrology and the science of *Feng Shui*, or geomancy, are in reality studies of the different expressions of *Qi;* astrology as it is involved in the heavens, and *Feng Shui* as it is expresses itself in lines of force or energy in the earth's crust.

The *I Ching*, the oldest of the Chinese classics, as shown in my previous work, and in the works of others, such as Master Ni Hua Ching, is actually a book of energetics demonstrating the regular flow of *Qi* throughout the world, and specifically as it affects human life. Each hexagram expresses three aspects of *Qi*: The top two lines are expressions of the heavenly or celestial energies; the bottom two the energies of the earth, and, finally, the middle two lines of the hexagram represent the human being who completes the universe with the expression of human energy.

The cycle of hexagrams reveal not only the cycles active in individual life, but also the grander cycles of human and universal history. The Chinese dynasties were associated with the cycles of the hexagrams and the elements corresponding at any one time to their energy. For example, the Ch'in Dynasty used black as its color, since the energies associated with the Ch'in were those of water and water corresponds to the color black.

▶ ▶

Lest it be assumed that this idea of *Qi*, or energy, is applied only to such endeavors as astrology, *Feng Shui*, and the *I Ching*, it is to be remembered that Chinese science and technology, which led the world until the late eighteenth century, were also based on the interactions of *Qi*. This is demonstrated by the Chinese development of magnetism far earlier and far beyond their European rivals.

Chinese science was developed most assiduously by the Taoists. Taoism, as will be discussed below, is a system of philosophy that takes nature as its model. For the Taoists, what is natural is good, what is artificial invariably gives rise to evil.[109] The study of nature was thus a matter of great importance to the Taoist sages, and the development of science, a logical extension and progression of their work.

Since, however, science was developed by people with a specific philosophical viewpoint, science, and specifically this science based on energetics, had an ethical content. Chinese philosophers, scientists, and physicians studied the interaction of *Qi* and developed theories of human disposition and behavior based on their observations.

Chinese medicine is specifically concerned with the *Qi* in the human body. The human being, however, as in the *I Ching*, includes the energies of heaven and earth and converts them to human *Qi*. Since the human being is composed of *Qi* and is, in fact, viewed as a pattern or matrix of *Qi* flow, there is again no sharp division between the mental and the physical. Both are merely differing expressions of *Qi*. Therefore, many of what Westerners would describe as physical ailments also have their mental components and vice versa. Any treatment applied to one part of the *Qi* field has remote effects on other parts of the field.

As with Christianity and Buddhism, the Chinese philosophers apply a medical model to behavior and consequently to ethics. Contaminated or poorly flowing *Qi* is concomitant with evil dispositions of mind and can lead to destructive behavior.[110] Accordingly, the physicians attempt to restore balance to the person by restoring balance to the *Qi* field.

Taking this a step further, since human beings can affect the situation of the *Qi* field, it is also possible for the individual to affect his or her own *Qi* field. The Chinese have two forms of practice that rely on the manipulation of *Qi: Qi Gong* and alchemy.

Qi Gong is the practice of utilizing breathing techniques, physical exercises, and meditation to increase the amount of *Qi* in the human body and to direct its flow. By doing so, the *Qi Gong* master cures and prevents diseases of the mind and body and acquires super-physical and mental strength and powers. If pursued diligently, the *Qi Gong* master may gain either Taoist or Buddhist enlightenment.[111]

Chinese alchemy, like that discussed by Carl Jung, is aimed specifically at changing the flow of *Qi* and by using its concentrated power, opening the channels between the denser physical body and the subtle energy body.[112] Gradually this energy body becomes so charged with *Qi* that it becomes the primary body of the alchemist and he or she becomes an Immortal.[113]

The principles of *Qi* usage are also basic to the Chinese martial arts, since an enhanced *Qi* flow provides strength, stamina, grace, and intuition.[114] Examples, of course, are *Taiji, Baqua,* and Iron Shirt *Qi Gong.* The martial arts model of dealing with force through absorption, redirection, or resistance mirrors the manners of handling evil, which is also a force. Evil can obviously be resisted, but evil can also be redirected, as in Jesus' statement to return good for evil and to pray for one's enemies. Evil can be absorbed as in turning the other cheek. These are all proven strategies for dealing with force. Therefore, the energy perspective of the Chinese — and for that matter of the Indians — and the martial arts model of ethics, is apropos. Indeed, many of the most devout Taoists and Buddhists throughout East Asia have traditionally been martial arts masters — and physicians.

At this point then it is an important to stop and note that while this "physical" or energy model of behavior is quite enlightening as to how ethical and non-ethical behavior and frames of mind occur, it really leaves us finally in a position similar to that of the West. All that has been accomplished has been to erase the rigid division between mind and body

— and maybe even spirit — but given that the quality, quantity, and flow of *Qi* determine the dispositions and behaviors of the human being, and, that these things can be changed, what makes the decision to change? Who or what is the actor or initiator, and can anything determine this actor? As with the West, the ultimate choices can never be explained. We are again in the mystical realm of the "person," or the Self; *Brahman/atman*.

Questions then must be raised of this Self. Is it by nature good, evil, or indifferent? Do these terms have any meaning when applied to a transcendental, undetermined, indefinable actor?

Chinese classical philosophy has dealt with this question of the natural essence of the human being from pre-history.

There is a Chinese children's book called the *Three Character Classic*, so called because each line contains three Chinese characters which when recited give the rhythmical effect that children find easy to remember. The first line of this book states, "The nature of man is originally good."[115]

Debate over human nature was a central matter for Chinese thought, and all positions were eventually taken. Mencius, Confucius' revered follower, argued that the human was composed of two parts: an animal part that is neither good nor evil, and the human part which, as the *Three Character Classic* states, is originally good.[116]

Although human nature is originally good, however, it can be corrupted by its environment and trained to be evil. That is why good government and education and compassion are so important to Confucians.

For Mencius, human nature contains the "beginnings" of virtue. These beginnings are actually feelings such as shame and dislike, modesty and yielding, right and wrong. These feelings through education and cultural cultivation develop into the virtues of righteousness, propriety, and wisdom.[117]

While Mencius represents the idealistic wing of Confucianism, there is another wing, that of the Li School, or the Realists. The Realists are represented by Hsun Tzu, who taught that the nature of the human being is originally evil.[118] However, being a Confucian, Hsun believed that education could make a person good.[119] Accordingly, Hsun taught that nature was evil and that only culture could make a person good. Value comes from culture.[120]

The problem with Hsun's position is that if humans are originally evil, how could a culture develop that was good? Han Fei Tzu, Hsun's student, solved this problem. He ignored it. To Han, who founded what was called the Legalist school, only law with its accompanying rewards and punishments made people good and society orderly.[121] This is a very positivistic and behavioristic view of humans and society.

For the Legalists, law not virtue was the basis of civilization. Whether human nature was good or evil was immaterial as long as the law was applied and obeyed consistently. Interestingly, from a modern Western perspective, the Chinese positions on human nature jibe very well with the management theories developed to explain the behavior of employees in a corporation. There are three theories of human behavior in corporations: Theory X, Theory Y, and from a Japanese prospective, Theory Z.[122] Theory X holds that human beings are basically lazy and evil and will work only when forced to. Money is the only reward granted for work.[123] This also calls for a very autocratic style of management. The employee is constantly watched and monitored and is given very little, if any, freedom of action. The classical assembly line is an example of Theory X management.

Theory Y holds that human beings are basically good, and that if given the chance they will work just to do a good job. Management in this type of company is very humanistic. The employee is treated well and money is not considered the reward, but instead the humanistic treatment and compliments from management are considered sufficient to motivate the individual.

Theory Z was developed by the Japanese. It argues that there must be a relationship of trust between management and employee. Trust is based on information. The more information that the employee is given the more the employee will be in a position to make the correct choices. Examples of this type of management, of course, would be the Japanese automobile companies and perhaps computer companies.[124]

As one can see, Theory X relates very well to the positions of the Realistic school of Confucianism, Theory Y, the school of Mencius, and, Theory Z to the ideas of Hsun Tzu in that education or information are the bases of good human behavior. There is obviously nothing new under the sun.

After the fall of the Ch'in Dynasty, which was dominated by the Legalists, Confucianism again became prominent under the Han Dynasty.[125] The outstanding thinker of this period was the scholar Tung Chung-Shu. Tung took the only remaining position concerning human nature, which is that human nature is neither good nor evil, but again, as a Confucian, it could be made good by education.

A final position is that of the Taoists. For the Taoists each person's nature is unique. Goodness is to follow one's nature or *Te* and give it free expression.[126] *Te* in this context can mean either power or virtue.[127] As one can see, the idea of *Qi* or energy fits very well with the philosophical term *Te*.

To the Taoist, nature itself is good and the artificial, including law and culture, is the root of all evil.[128] If a human acts according to his or her *Te*, he will never go wrong. In order to do this, he or she must withdraw either physically or mentally from entanglements in the world.[129] Where the Confucian emphasized education to develop human nature, the Taoist argued for a "cultivated ignorance."[130]

As time went on, Neo-Confucian and Neo-Taoist thinkers borrowed from each other and fabricated an eclectic style of philosophy.[131] Both Mencius and the Taoists, for instance, seemed to be saying that human nature is originally good. They differ only in how that nature is to be developed. Mencius and the Confucians assert through education and culture, the Taoists through withdrawal and contemplation.

This almost brings us back full circle to Plato. Given that the human being is composed of some sort of physical vehicle, a body, a pattern of energy vibrations, and that vehicle includes both mind and body and, a part that is indefinable and transcends or goes beyond the everyday world, whether this thing is a "self," *atman/Brahman*, or "person," if this being is undetermined, how can it have a "nature"? On the other hand, if it does have a "nature," how can that nature be called "good" or "evil"? The Chinese seem to define the human being in ethical rather than metaphysical terms. However, what does this mean? If the human is originally good, does this refer to substance, things, or essence as per Plato, or does it require the acting out of this goodness as per Mencius and the Chinese philosophers? Since people do not always act good, or evil for that matter, but are stated to be originally good or evil, their "nature" must be similar, though more immanent than Plato or Aristotle's ideas. Again, however, what does "good" or "evil" mean? Apparently, if the terms are to have any meaning, that meaning is discovered in actions displayed in the world. But again that assumes we know already what good and evil are and begs the question. We are back to Plato. We will try to answer these questions in bioenergetic terms in our discussion of virtue and its expressions.

A being, such as the human being, is such that part of him or her transcends and is not bound by the world. Therefore, their being is potentially to act in any way possible within the bounds of physical circumstances. Unless there is some sort of external constraint, the human being is free to act in any way it chooses. This follows from our study of the human being, what we have discovered the human being to be. However, morality, art, knowledge, etc., must come from the human being or at least be able to be understood by the human being. Freedom implies choice but not necessity. Perhaps, therefore, Tung is correct in asserting that human nature is neither originally good, nor originally evil. The application of the terms "good" or "evil" must, therefore, come from some sort of external, that is, non-human standard. They can accordingly be utilitarian, that is, any action that helps the survival and comfort of the greatest number of human beings, which would include the views of Hobbes, Bentham, and Marx. Or, the external rules are arbitrary and serve whatever end the ruler makes, be he king, dictator, or mob. Finally, the external definitions of morality can come from revealed religion, Moslem, Hindu, Christian, Jewish — any group that claims to have a direct pipeline to God as embodied in written scriptures or traditional modes of behavior. If one thinks clearly about it, these three standards tend to overlap in effect; only their sources of authority are distinct.

In other words, nothing in the make-up of the human being as analyzed in this chapter requires the human being to act in any predictable, determined, or consistent manner. That the human being can be made to do so under certain controlled circumstances for brief periods of time in no way vitiates the essential human freedom to act perversely. Since the human being is essentially free, except for the certain amount of physical constraint inherent in embodiment, the human being in itself can be neither good nor evil, since good and evil are terms imposed from the application of external standards. All external standards imply arbitrariness from the human perspective and are inhuman since they necessarily restrict human freedom which is synonymous with human nature or, more accurately, human being.

Now it is acceptable that the laws of physics impinge upon the human body and restrict human freedom, since the laws of physics are non-human by definition. Further, the advice that one should be moderate in one's habits is also an inhuman prescription since it is based on chemical laws, such as the effect of the dehydration of the body through excessive alcohol use. The human being has and is a body, but calling something such as the injunction to moderation moral is no better than making the laws of biology synonymous with morality. Perhaps this is the position of the Taoist. Nature as goal. Imitate nature and one will lead a good life. However, Taoism has developed beyond mere imitation, as will be seen, and "nature" is a broader term than that conceived by both the Empiracists and the Rationalists.

Given our analysis of the human being, the question may fairly be raised as to whether the human being can in any human way be moral. And if the human being can be moral, how can he or she be so? The human being is both free and embodied. The only things prohibited by these two conditions are those things prohibited to the body by natural law, that is the laws of physics, chemistry, and biology. But are there any things allowed by these conditions? The answer is yes, and the answer comes from Hegel and Marx. The human being is embodied in the physical world so that he or she is free and able, thanks to embodiment, to create and produce. The only possibility for moral action exists in human creativity and the world-transforming power of production.

If one is to be judged as a human being, one can only be judged on what and how one creates and produces. This is the only criterion that grows out of the twofold natures of freedom and embodiment. In other words, the human, because of his or her nature, can only be judged as an artist.

This position also comports with the view of the human as an energy field, á la the Chinese and Hindus. The nature of energy also is to do work. If one were to ask why the human, a free and transcendent being, is embodied, the answer would be so that he or she would have the energy necessary to fulfill his or her nature; that is, to create, produce, and work. The essence of the human, both body and world, is creation.

What is creation? Creation is to take what is given, and by using and changing it, to produce something different, including the given. However, the element of freedom must be added so as to make the work something more than a mere combination. Freedom plus physicality makes the resulting entity a human product, a creation, a work of art. The human being must fuse his or her freedom to the world.

At this point one may well inquire as to just how creativity is to be judged if, in fact, it is the basis not only of human being, but of both art and ethics? An attempt will be made to answer the question later in this book. For the moment, however, our goal has been to examine the nature of the human being and its relationship to the nature of ethics. We stated that the nature of the human being is to create. We also stated that the nature of ethics was conflict. It is conflict which raises ethical questions to the level of consciousness. Is the above assessment of ethics consistent with our examination of the human being?

We have stated that creation is the addition of human freedom to the given world. The world, as we know from our analysis of science, is composed of "things" and exists in the past. The world, however, is not simply composed of things. Because of the embodiment of the human being, the world also exists alongside; against the human being. Due to embodiment, the world is also always present to the human. The body gives presence. It makes a present time dimension. As such, it impinges upon human freedom. This is a constant state of conflict and keeps human energy in a state of tension until relieved, temporarily, by creative activity.

Following Sartre, who defines the human as the being who constantly says "no" to the "what is" of the world, the human, in order to fulfill his or her nature, rejects the world as it presently is and enters into conflict with it, directing his or her energy to creating something new and human. The human foresees what is possible from the world's raw materials and works through time to produce something that will exist in the future. Human freedom adds a future to the world.

In order to create, the human being must foresee what is possible. In order to foresee, the human must have his or her attention drawn to a given situation. Energy must be directed towards that situation. This can only occur consciously and intentionally. If not, freedom has not been involved, and any result is simply chance, not human creation nor, as such, human being. Nothing, as Jung has observed, draws consciousness and produces psychic energy like opposition.[132] Synonymous terms are irritation and conflict.

Opposition and conflict cause human creativity. Human creativity is the source of art and morality. We arrive back at studying the nature of ethics by applying the models of conflict, which is *Budo*.

In the next chapter we will examine the otherness that opposes human freedom as one half of the process of creativity. We will study otherness under the guise of the Confucian term *Ming*, which can be translated as fate, or, that over which one has no control. After examining creation in its aspect as *Ming* or opposition, we will develop the internal response to *Ming*, which is virtue. Virtue will be seen in the ancient martial guise of "strength." Virtue is the manner

▶▶

one uses in meeting fate or *Ming*. From there we will look to the application of virtue to fate in the practice of *Budo*, the art of the warrior. Finally, we will examine how *Budo* can be applied to both professional and everyday life.

CHAPTER TWO

Fate: Knowing Ming

When I graduated from law school in 1981, I landed a job in a corporate legal department. I didn't fit. After a year, I hung out my shingle in front of the old frame house my wife and I bought in a blue-collar neighborhood. Then we learned my wife was pregnant. Losing my corporate job really made her day.

At any rate, I met clients in my den, and strangely enough, made enough money to pay my share of our expenses. Being a solo practitioner, however, I did not have the luxury of turning down any clients — no matter how crooked, demented, or weird.

One day I got a referral from the local Bar Association. Of course, I took it. Several hours later, an old man with a pointed white beard arrived at my door. He used a cane and, except for the fact that he was dressed in sports clothes, looked like Monty Wooley in *The Man Who Came to Dinner*. Unfortunately, my client, unlike the late Mr. Wooley, was totally insane.

Our conversation began with a discussion of how the Dayton police had a secret file on him. Then how the CIA had done illegal experiments on him when he was in the Army. He gave me books to read about these experiments. He also gave me cash. My full fee. Up front. I was all ears. Damn CIA! How dare they!

The actual case this gentleman came to discuss with me was an automobile accident. A delivery service driver had swerved while passing on a curve and had hit my client's car. As a result, my client suffered whiplash injuries. Damn delivery service driver! I told my wife to go to the bank.

The only catch was that the client, who had been through three other attorneys — a bad sign — had failed to answer a set of interrogatories that the kindly insurance company lawyer had dumped on him. It was late Friday afternoon, and he had to have the answers submitted to the company *before* Monday.

I called the law firm representing the company. No, Mr. So-and-So had already left, and they were closing. Too bad, I said. I have an express package for him. Is anybody there on Saturday? Why, of course. Normally secretaries came in to finish work left over from the week. There's a side door! Just ring!

So we spent the next three hours lying on the floor with legal papers spread everywhere. We finished at 9:00. The next morning I rang the bell at the law firm and handed a not-too-happy secretary the completed interrogatories. Presto! We were still in the case. Now we were sure to have a trial! A trial??? I had never done a trial and now I was taking on one of the largest law firms in the area — lawyers, secretaries, paralegals, paramilitary, demolition experts, hitmen (I had seen too many movies) from my den.

Monday morning, myself and the well-dressed, clean-shaven, clean-smelling, friend-of-the-judge insurance lawyer met the judge to set a trial date. Both the insurance lawyer and the judge had thought this had gone away thanks to their before Monday trick. (The secretary who told me about the side door was found by fishermen.) They were not exactly hostile at this meeting, but, I'm not on anyone's Christmas card list.

Reality now began to crash in. Trial was in three weeks. The case itself was three years old, a cold case. I frantically began calling the doctors and chiropractors who had treated my client. I spent hours interviewing them. I engaged an engineer to explain the physics of cars on a curve like the one involved in the accident. I contacted the witnesses listed in the accident report. All of this in addition to answering the barrage of neatly-typed memoranda that poured into my mailbox on a daily basis from the insurance lawyer's firm, questioning my evidence, questioning my legal theories, my parentage, my sexuality, my species — well, you get it.

I was working twenty-hour days. I slept at the law library a couple of nights. The day before trial — my first trial — arrived. I was exhausted and almost ready. I sped around town in my 1968 Oldsmobile conducting final interviews with witnesses and writing memoranda in my head. There was so much to do. The appointments were only ten to fifteen minutes apart — all day. On the way to one critical medical meeting, my car ran out of gas. I was stranded. It started to rain. I had no gas can and no money on me. I had to go to the bathroom. It took an hour to get back on the road. I was late for the rest of the day, but keeping up my nerve, I made all of the appointments.

I arrived home exhausted on the night before my first trial. But I had done good work. My wife, who had had a bad day at work, and then with our two toddlers, was not disposed to give sympathy. I sat down to eat a warmed-over supper of macaroni and tuna when the phone rang. It was my client's former lawyer. The former lawyer informed me that he had mistakenly gotten a call from one of my eye-witnesses who said that my client had offered him money to describe the accident so as to put the blame on the other side. This witness said that, if called, he would tell the Court. By the way, if I didn't call the judge and disclose this, the attorney would.

I was destroyed. First trial, weeks of work resuscitating a dead case and then this! I called the judge and the insurance lawyer at home on a Monday night. They were just thrilled to hear from me. The man would have to be called to testify and would speak of the money my client offered him. But, due to the rules of ethics, I could not withdraw. I love the law. Glad I became a lawyer.

To top off my evening, I found a new memorandum from the insurance company on my desk, which needed an immediate answer. It was now 10:00 p.m. I kissed my delighted wife and headed for the law library. As I settled down to a long bout of critical research ... the law library caught on fire! We were all forced to leave. I'm not making this up. It is true.

I finished my research early the next morning and started what would be a six-day trial — which I lost. I didn't take the hint when my client talked about the CIA. I didn't take the hint when my car ran out of gas. I didn't take the hint when my client tried to pay off a witness. But I should have taken the hint when the law library caught on fire. The Fates did not want me on this case. But I am Eastern European. I am dense.

I use the term "fate" in recounting this story to illustrate that there are some things over which one simply has no control. One has the freedom, as a human being, to react, but one has no control over the events and forces that intervene in and act on one's life. This lack of control is undoubtedly the basis of all the many forms of fortune-telling, and, indeed, of all human endeavors that attempt to predict and direct the future. Included in these attempts are science and religion. Only art does not make such an attempt. Though possibly existing in the future, art contemplates only the present. That is, it comtemplates only its own immediate presentation.

In the last chapter we found that a human being was composed of three "parts": a physical body which is another object or "thing" among other "things" in the world subject to the laws of physics; an individual human body which exists in the world, but is a "quasi-object" since, unlike other true objects, it cannot be "gotten rid of" and, it is assumed and peripheral in all acts of the human being, and, finally; a mysterious, indefinable "person" that is one's pure subjectivity, but which ultimately overflows the boundary of the subject and object, transcending them both and endowed with the power to say "no" the to given; to what is.

In the last chapter we also argued that science dealt in objects, "things." Since "things" were necessarily complete, or at least defined as such in order to permit study, it was argued that science was concerned with the past.

However, this assessment of science is not entirely correct. In order to study an object, it is true that science must delimit it. But the process does not stop there. In order to be of any use whatsoever, science must be able to predict. In other words, if an object is exposed to force X, then result Y will occur. This, of course, adds a future dimension to science.

It is important to note, however, that the scientific "future" is not the future of common experience. The future for science is the future of the controlled experiment. The present situation, the object, must be strictly controlled and limited. It is a completed "thing." The force or object that acts upon it is likewise rigidly controlled. Finally, the predicted outcome must itself be severely limited or the experiment is questionable.

Fortune-telling and magic, out of which experimental science eventually grew,[133] shares with science the need for prediction and control of the future. The very human reason for these activities is a fear of and an endeavor to control "fate." The human being, just as Scrooge in *A Christmas Carol* fears the future most of all. The basis for this fear is the simple fact that except within certain narrow limits, the future cannot be controlled or predicted. It is the unknown. The fear of the dark.

Nietzsche argued that in order for human culture and society to be possible, humans needed to develop a memory. That is the reason for primitive laws with their harsh punishments. Punishments provided fear and respect. Punishments provided the force necessary to make the memory work.[134] However, all that memory creates is ritual. One remembers how one acted to avoid punishment and simply and invariably repeats that behavior. Superstition is the by-product of ritual and memory. Superstition occurs when an action, unrelated causally to the desired result, is mistakenly believed to have helped in the cause and is thus repeated along with the actual causal behavior. An example would be wearing a pair of "lucky" socks when one plays softball. One gets a hit by swinging the bat correctly and connecting with the ball. The "lucky" socks are simply a superstition. Memory alone cannot separate out the non-essential elements of the activity. Experimentation, that is, a future, is needed in order to do that. Memory and ritual leave no room for adaptation. New situations must be ignored or ineffectively met. With memory and ritual, the future is defined as being completely encompassed by the past.

Although science continues to question the past and the present, and, at least tacitly conceives of a partially unknown future, it does not contemplate an unknowable future. Science necessarily moves with the idea that all activity is lawful, and, therefore, can be known. It differs from ritual only in the acknowledgement that the breadth of possible but knowable behavior or situations is much wider than that entertained by ritual — but not infinite. The narrow circumspection of the possible future in experimental design, allowing for only one acceptable outcome, is phenomenologically equivalent to ritual, however. Science, like ritual, implicitly accepts the idea that if one has A and does B, then C and only C will ever result.

Modern science has, of course, progressed beyond the narrowly ritualistic and mechanistic science of the early modern era by using the laws of probability and statistics. Again, however, while this approach allows for more flexibility in its results, and recognizes chance in its world-view, the basic need to make behavior "lawful" maintains the relationship of science and ritual. The concepts of "law" and ritual are congruent.

The primitive "laws" of any people have to do with performance of rituals. Look to the *Old Testament, Deuteronomy, Numbers,* etc. Look to the *Vedas.* Look also to the Chinese classics. The minute directions for the performance of ritual are the first matters codified. They are followed shortly by domestic matters and real estate — which are themselves ritualized. Witness *Livery of Seisin* under the old Anglo Saxon land laws.

The concepts of "law" and "lawful" are, therefore, derived from ritual. Ritual itself is likely to have been derived from biology, from instinct. When mating, animals dance, move, posture, and perform in rigid, inflexible ways. Territoriality is established in much the same way. Defense and aggression also involve pre-patterned and invariable displays of behavior. That such behaviors are "ritualistic" is underscored by

▸▸

the fact, presented by the Biological Rationalists mentioned in the first chapter, that species fail to adapt. They die out. The ritual does not vary, but the environment does.

Law, therefore, social as well as physical, is associated with ritual, with memory, and with the past. Morality and ethics, on the other hand, are not. Morality goes beyond law, as will be seen below.

Science, as we have stated, is an attempt to control and predict the future. Its basic motive is not curiosity but fear. We want to explain away the giant gila monster that the natives swear lives deep in the jungle and carries off cattle at night. "Silly native superstition Carruthers, old boy." But Carruthers always gets eaten. Science wants to make the future a "thing" just like the past. The problem is that there is no final or convincing proof that the world is lawful. One has only to read David Hume's criticisms of the "laws" of cause and effect to get a feeling for the elusiveness of law.

Hume was a consistent empiricist and argued that all that we can "know" comes from sense and mental impressions. These impressions are distinct and constantly arise and pass away. Hume accordingly began by arguing that none of these impressions taken by itself implies the existence of any others nor does the non-existence of anything contradict the existence of any other thing. If we saw fire without smoke, the mere absence of smoke would not mean that the fire was not burning. Therefore we go beyond the evidence of the senses by using the idea of cause and effect. Hume asserts that the belief that one thing necessarily follows another is based on the "supposition that the future resembles the past."[135] To this Hume counters that there is no definite proof that this should be so. How then do human beings come to believe that the "future resembles the past"?

Hume states that the answer lies in psychology. We perceive that event B always occurs after event A. There is no reason that this should be so, but like Pavlov's dogs, after a period of time when we see event A, our mind by habit jumps to event B.[136] As an empiricist, Hume is consistent in finding nothing in the passing impressions, or in the mind itself that requires the idea of causation. However, he recognizes that as human beings we could not function without these habits and the accompanying, but unjustified idea of cause and effect. Hume also finds that memory played a great part in all of this.[137]

We are back to ritual. Perhaps it is no small wonder that the Confucian classics place such emphasis on ceremony — including religious ceremony — even though the Confucians had no belief in a personal god. Ceremony, ritual, is performed for its own sake to train the mind to behave in a law-like manner. Let's pretend.

Anglo-American law is based on "precedent." Again we have the belief that the "future resembles the past." If that were true, however, we would not have law libraries bursting with volumes of case law. Precedents are applied to new cases, but the precedents rarely ever fit the facts. Therefore, the law is extended, "interpreted," bent, to fit an infinite and unpredictable variety of facts. Because of the nature of human beings, as seen in the preceding chapter, nowhere is it more apparent that the future need not resemble the past than in the study of human affairs.

Human behavior has long been considered incapable of being studied "scientifically"[138] since it cannot be subjected to laboratory conditions, that is, the possible variables and, the possible outcomes produced by the variables, cannot be rigidly enough controlled so as to produce an unquestionable result.

Accordingly, social scientists have either narrowed the behaviors they study to the most reflexive and mechanical, or, have relied upon statistics. We have already dealt with the criticisms of the narrow behavioristic approach by pointing out that by only permitting the study of single, reflexive behavior, the human part of the human being, his or her higher functions, are precisely what are eliminated from consideration. Further, since we are dealing with thinking human beings, the experimental subject's interpretations and motivations in response to stimuli must be considered, and may very well differ from those of the experimenter, thus invalidating the experiment even though the expected behavior occurred.[139] Finally, in real-world situations, and, even occasionally in the experimental setting, the human being can both "cheat" and act perversely, that is, act in a manner inconsistent with the hypothesis, just to be a stinker.

Science then is a very limited and ineffectual way of controlling and predicting the future. It is active in that it is derived from ritual and magic, but like ritual and magic its main value is to demonstrate just how very difficult it is to control or predict even a small slice of the future. Its very premise, that the "future resembles the past" is highly questionable.

More open-minded and flexible than science and ritual are the various forms of fortune-telling. In true fortune-telling, some form of chance is incorporated into the process of "reading" the future. For example, coins or yarrow sticks are tossed to read the *I Ching*.[140] While the rules of interpretation are fairly fixed based on pre-determined configurations of symbols, the actual falling of the coins, sticks, etc., is by chance. Obviously, as with life itself, and under the laws of probability, the number of possible combinations of factors is innumerable. The difference, however, is that, rather than projecting from the past and present into the future, the configuration of coins, cards, etc., is produced in the present, but according to the underlying premise of fortune-telling is actually a picture, a "snapshot" of the future. It is the future acting on the present.

For example, I shuffle a deck of Tarot cards. I deal a magic cross spread. It contains thirteen cards taken at random. Whether the cards are upright or reversed is also taken into account. Cards one and two, dealt in the present, represent an interpretation of the past. Card three, dealt in the present, represents the present. Cards four and five represent opposing forces. Cards six and seven, one's hopes and expectations; one's own mental projection into the future. Cards eight through thirteen, dealt in the present, represent a picture of the future.[141] Other spreads break the future into near and distant. Some give more cards to the present.[142] The point is that except for the readings of the configurations, which are fairly set, there is no underlying assumption that the future will resemble the past. In fortune-telling, the future is discovered first in the present, and then the past is made to conform to the future. The process in science is just the opposite. A half-way house between science and fortune-telling is astrology. Like fortune-telling, astrology assumes that the future can be known in the present. However, its variables, the celestial objects, are not as many as some other forms of fortune-telling. For example, the Tarot deck contains seventy-eight cards. Given the numbers of positions in a spread and its consideration of upright or reversed placings, plus the fact that the cards can be dealt as many times as one wants, the possibilities are infinite in a purely mathematical sense.

Astrology deals with ten celestial bodies, twelve signs and twelve houses. There are also perhaps eight to ten "angles" or aspects between these bodies that are considered significant. Obviously, the significant "pictures" that one produces by astrology change more slowly than the shuffling of a deck of cards or the tossing of coins. Further, they cannot be altered by a human actor.

While astrology shares with fortune-telling the assumption that the future can be known in the present, it shares with science the assumption that the future resembles the past, since chance is not involved in the positioning of the planets. Planetary positions have been projected and calculated since the most ancient of times. Knowledge of the positions of the celestial bodies in the past and present does allow one to predict their positions in the future. Since the basic interpretation of the planetary positions are established, the predictions based upon them do rigidly resemble the past.

An underlying inference that can be made from the assumptions of both science and fortune-telling is that at least the past and the future are things. In other words, to predict it the future must already exist. Just like Yellowstone Park where I will be vacationing this summer, it exists already; I simply have to go there. Time under both disciplines is seen in *spatial* terms. We shall return to this point, but must examine one more view of the future, that of revealed religion.

What I mean by revealed religion in our present discussion is any form of worship based upon a personal communication from God to humans which is reduced to scripture and, most importantly, which makes specific predictions about the future history of the world. Such religions are essentially Western and include Christianity and Islam most prominently. Judaism also deals in prediction, but does not, at least in the *Old Testament* itself, make predictions as to the ultimate end of the world.

Judaism does contain a prophetic tradition. Predictions are made concerning the future of dynasties, peoples, and specific rulers. Further predictions are made concerning a coming Messiah and the resurrection of the Kingdom of Israel. While based on moral, or, at least legalistic underpinnings, these prophesies are essentially naturalistic and this-worldly.

Christianity, which was born in the Jewish milieu, reinterpreted the Jewish scriptures and added historical predictions of its own. Embracing all peoples, Christianity projected a specific end to the world and a specific future history both cosmic and political. Christianity did not attempt to predict everything concerning the future, nor does it provide a system or procedure that just anyone can use to make specific predictions. Instead, since Christianity is concerned only with human relationships with God, it only provides, once and for all, specific pictures of specific events essential to that relationship. These predictions were recorded in the past, but are valid for the future and inalterable.

Likewise with Islam. The end of the world and the description of future life are repeatedly given. Examples are taken from the past — the scriptures of Judaism and Christianity — to demonstrate what Allah can and will do with the world. The revelation is given in the past, and thus, under the theory of revealed religion, the future, cannot be altered.

Under revealed religion then, a part of the future can be known by anyone simply by reading the scripture. There is no process involved as in fortune-telling and science, and no chance or probability. The significant part of the future is

▶▶

revealed. Dictated.

Again, as with fortune-telling, there is no assumption that the future resembles the past. However, revealed religion is based upon the premise that God creates the future just as He did the past, and views the future as present. Therefore, revealed religion, just as with science and fortune-telling, sees time as a "thing."

This brings us back to our original point of departure for this chapter: Fate. If the future can be known, it already exists. Even science, with its recent inclusion of the fourth dimension and hyperspace, tacitly recognizes the logic of this assertion. Religion sees it from the perspective of an all-knowing God. "Predestination" is a Christian term, but also in the *Qur'an*, Allah states that He will mislead whom He will; that He already knows the final fates of all people.

Fortune-telling, by incorporating chance into the process, seems strangely enough to be the least determined of these approaches. However, the very premise of "reading" the future indicates that the future somehow already exists in order to enable it to be "read" in the present.

This raises several related questions concerning fate: What are the consequences of viewing time as a "thing"? What are the consequences of "knowing" the future? What are the moral consequences of these two propositions? What is the nature of fate? How does one act in the face of fate?

In answer to our first question, "What are the consequences of viewing time as a thing," it would appear that just like a block of wood or a moon rock we could potentially know everything about the future as well as the past. Everything would be completely determined. Is this really the case, however?

First, the future as well as the past, is so vast, so intricate, and so long that it may very well be at once totally determined and unknowable. The universe at any one moment is set. If we could stop time, it would appear to be theoretically possible to "know" the entire universe. But this would be a mistaken impression. The great immensity, indeed the infinity of all of its parts, would preclude the possibility of total knowledge, even with infinite time available.

Further, following Kant, and Kierkegaard for that matter, the instrument for processing and storing this infinity of knowledge is the human mind. As pointed out by these two gentlemen, this mind, although immense in its capacity, is nonetheless finite. It can conceive of the infinite, but it cannot encompass the infinite itself.

Finally, time itself would be required to examine time. If one wished, for God knows what reason, to examine a football field, it would take time to walk from one end to the other. If time itself were conceived of as a thing, like the football field, some sort of hypertime would be required to traverse it. This brings in an infinite regress, and as such is absurd and pointless.

It may be countered, however, that if one were to move along the fourth or time dimension, the three spatial dimensions would collapse into one point, just as time itself is viewed as one from the perspective of the three spatial dimensions. In short, all of space would collapse into a single point that could be viewed instantaneously. However, again this does not negate the Kantian and Kierkegaardian positions, and again the question is raised as to whether the finite brain would still be capable of encompassing a point which contains the entire universe. The entire universe is still there, just in an infinitely dense state.

Additionally, the viewer is a part of the thing being viewed. As a completed thing, there can be no movement. Therefore, the actual viewing involved may still very well be limited to the confines of one's original, invariable place in the universe. That is, one could possibly view one's own life and circumstances, but without the potential for movement, be unable to view and thus "know" anything else.

An answer to these two problems could, however, be made from the prospective of the philosophies of the human being. As we know from our examination of the human being, there is a recognized part that transcends the limits of the individual and, indeed, of the universe itself. This is the *atman/Brahman*, soul, or person that we have discussed. These parts of the human being are by definition infinite in that they are not bounded by the world. They contain all possibilities. Therefore, they are potentially able to encompass the infinite.

Two objections, however, can be raised to this gambit. First, we are talking about knowledge. Knowing the future; knowing the universe. Knowledge, by definition, is a function of the human mind, or at least it must be filtered through it to have any sense or meaning. We are back again to the finite. Second, the old Thomistic problem recurs: Since the human being must exist in the world, or at least partially so to be human, by detaching a part of the human being from the world, the result is non-human. Therefore, the human being must be destroyed as a human being to encompass the infinite. But morality and ethics, the focus of our inquiry, are human endeavors, and as such cannot be derived from the non-human. Laws can. Ethics cannot. Therefore, this appeal to the infinite in the human being fails.

One final point needs to be made in this matter. All of what has been said concerning the future can be applied to the past. Yes, more of the past is viewable by the human being, but the past, too, is infinite. Likewise, it is subject to our limited field of view, and likewise, is it subject to the vagaries and vicissitudes of the human body and mind.

In answer to our first question then, even if the universe, including time, were a thing, it would be theoretically complete, but still unknowable to the limited human being. Fate, as the unknowable but inalterable, remains.

The second question is: "What are the consequences of knowing the future?" As can be seen this is not dependent upon, nor is it a possible query, under the concept of time being a thing. However, it should nonetheless be examined.

Perhaps although it is not possible to "know" the entire future or the entire past, a human being could "travel" somehow in time and view a circumscribed part of the future as in the present. This, after all, is very similar to the premises of fortune-telling. If this were possible, then significant parts of the future could be known. Further, this "travel" theory does not contradict the idea of time as a thing. It simply recognizes that the human being is finite, with a limited field of perception, and, tends to exist in the present. Again, of course, we would face the problems of detaching the human being from the space-time-mental continuum, or the "things," that is, the universe.

Maybe some sort of vision, or "seeing" such as the oracles of old were said to do would be a better way of viewing this matter. An extra-temporal sense of sight could be employed. In that respect no movement out of one's position in the space-time-mental continuum would be necessary. The time frame would also be that of the present viewing the future. The vision involved would also be finite, or limited, and, the human being could continue to exist in the present, in the world. Under this model it would be possible to "know" the future, or, a limited part of it.

On the face of it this present knowledge of the future would seem to give one an advantage in one's affairs. Surely if one knew what was going to happen one would be able to take advantage of this knowledge. This, of course, supposes that one could alter the future.

But if the future or time itself is a completed "thing," the idea of altering it is self-contradictory. Absurd. Perhaps, however, time and history are more like a living organism than a concrete thing. Parts of the organism could conceivably change their behavior and thereby alter the organism itself. This sounds plausible, but again its effects are not at all helpful. If a part of a united and dependently functioning organism suddenly changes its behavior, it necessarily affects other parts of the organism to which it is related. The changes in these parts may very well affect others. Since the goal of changing the part's behavior is to change the overall shape of the organism, one cannot, with one's finite perspective, determine all of the effects upon the infinite numbers of parts and processes in the universe. Therefore, if one could "see" a certain future, and then with this knowledge, change one's part in it, one would have to act first, and then either wait for the results or look again in the future to "see" the new configuration. Due to the infinity of parts and connections to the universe, one could not predict before changing one's behavior what the new future shape of the universe would be. And after acting, one would again have to "look" to see the results which, due to the infinity of the universe, would be a surprise, and, perhaps not at all what one intended. This does not nullify the possibility of "seeing" the future and acting to change it, but it does nullify any possible usefulness of such a procedure. Again, acting "blindly," one is left to the whims of chance. Fate. Knowledge of the future is possible, but not very useful.

One final perspective on the problem of seeing the future and acting upon it is that raised by Sartre. The human being is finite; not just spatially, but temporally. Since he or she only has a certain amount of time, that allotted time is constantly changing into the past, where it becomes ossified. As a human being makes choices, he or she precludes other possibilities; other possible futures. Accordingly, even if one could see the future and change one's behavior, one's range of possible choices would continually narrow until the possible future would come to a point and only one possible future would be left. Life in this respect is like a chess game. One makes moves, but by the logic of the game, after any move only certain other moves remain open to the player. Eventually all possible moves are made and the game ends. Under this scenario then, even if it were possible to change the future, the range of change is extremely limited and inevitably non-existent. Like the chess game, and, consistent with Sartre's observation, one's continuing behaviors do not free one, but instead unrelentingly enslave one. Fate, under this model, is like a python constricting a mouse-one becomes suffocated by it. Given the fact that the future, and the past for that matter, can in no way be practically known or such knowledge be useful, what are the moral consequences?

In the first place, the human being, just as the prosecutors at the beginning of Chapter One, cannot know the ultimate consequences of his or her actions. Further, due to the finite nature of human vision, both temporally and, if possible, extra-temporally, the human being can never know all of the forces acting upon any one moment or place in the space-time-mental continuum. Since this is true, how can a human being morally judge his or her actions? Is there any ultimate moral code possible for such a finite being? Is there any action that can satisfy all of the variables at any one place in the space-time-mental continuum?

The simple answer is that no human being can know what is ultimately right in any situation. The ancient scriptures are correct in this context: left to him or herself, the human is ignorant of good and evil. Apparently, an external source is needed, just as in the story in Genesis, to provide rules, a code, for human good and evil. But this gives rise to a contradiction: The human, being finite, cannot know good and evil on his or her own and thus requires a code, a law, to provide guidance. But law is a species of ritual. It assumes that the future resembles the past and that, therefore, the same behavior will fit all possible situations. However, the future may or may not be a determined "thing" and, even if it is, it does not necessarily follow that any one part resembles any other. Therefore, there is no guarantee that positive law is applicable.

An even greater contradiction arises in the nature of the human being: A part of the human exists in the world, but there is a part that exists beyond the world and is undetermined by it. This is the mystical person, soul, or *Brahman/atman*. As such, the human being has the power to negate the world as it is and thus is essentially free. Accordingly, laws apply to "things" which are complete and can never vary. Choice and negation are not qualities of "things." But they are of human beings. Human beings have the choice to assent to or reject laws and, therefore, to contradict the very nature of law. There are and can be, therefore, no real laws for human beings.

The human being is incapable of knowing good and evil. Nor is law, divine or otherwise, applicable to human beings and is, in fact, contradictory of human being. The human being, however, must live in the world to be human, a world in which he or she can have only limited knowledge and control, and to which only physical laws loosely and metaphorically apply. This lack of knowledge and control is called Fate. It is represented in mythology by wild, fearsome, and irrational beings who relentlessly pursue the human. Fear is the emotion they evoke.

Since humans must nonetheless live in this world and under these circumstances, fate must always be considered in any human endeavor, and no place more so than in the pursuit of morality and ethics. Fate is the given of the world, what the human being must work with. A closer examination is necessary.

This brings us to our fourth question: "What is the nature of fate?" We have tentatively defined fate as the unknowable and uncontrollable. In other words, there is the human being; a composite of body-mind and person-*Brahman/ atman*, and, there is the world. Fate acts on the human being in the world, or rather through the world and only through the world. The transcendental part of the human is undetermined and unlimited. Accordingly, it can be affected by nothing. However, since the human being as a human being must be a composite, it must, in one end of the continuum that is a human being, be affected by Fate. Again, since limits and boundaries, that is things and forces are only found in the world, Fate can only act on the human in the part of his or her being that is in the world.

Having said this, however, it is nonetheless not all that apparent how and where Fate acts upon the human being. Is Fate a "thing" in the world? It uses "things" such as the piano that falls from its pulley and hits me on the head; or the bacteria that infects my body and causes disease. But Fate itself, like gravity, is a force and is unobservable apart from its effect. Just as our knowledge of gravity could not exist apart from all of the falling apples of the world, Fate would be unknown except for all of the falling passenger jets of the world.

Since everything in the world can be "objectified," made into a "thing" by a human, as our discussion of the behavioral psychologists and empirical philosophers indicated, the encroachment of Fate comes to the very door of the transcendental person, swallowing and using both the human body and the human mind. It cannot, however, engulf the transcendental person which is not a thing as our studies have shown, and thus, the person can never be totally at the mercy of Fate.

So there are two components of being in the world: The transcendent person, and, Fate. Both components act upon the human mind and body. Again, the human mind/body is the halfway house, the battle ground, between these two forces.

It is tempting at this point to divide the world along partisan lines, that is the person and everything else. In other words, the person and the Other. The Other is defined here as anything that is not the transcendent person, anything against which the person must act. This, of course, is the basis of much of religion and occultism, especially those religions based on Gnostic principles which see the world as an alien place in which man is a stranger and is not at home.[143] However, this would be inaccurate since it would make Fate coterminous with the world.

The "things" of the world are basically neutral. They do not act upon the human being except to limit him or her. They are suffocating and irritating, but they have no ability to act on their own. They are passive. They can be manipulated and acted upon. This maleability is the basis of all of the aesthetic philosophy from Hegel to Nietzsche, and especially that of Marx.

But this position fails to recognize that there is something in the world actively working independently of a person's wishes. Fate exists independently of the person and is other than human. It works according to its own pressures and manipulates objects on an equal footing with the person. Life in the world thus becomes very much like a game between two opponents. They may or may not be equally matched and neither can completely read the other's mind nor prevent the other's move. Further, either party is free to act in an irrational manner. The game of life, in this context, is very much like the game of *Go*. It is not like chess, since chess becomes irreparably limited with each move, and leaves little room for freedom of action. *Go*, while eventually deterministic, deals in patterns and gives wider scope for freedom of action, and, the ability to reverse situations.

But I love the game of *Go* and I digress. The model nonetheless holds. Fate is a force that uses the "things" of the world just as the person uses them. It is unknowable and uncontrollable just as is the person. The world of things is the game board affected by the two forces — the transcendent person, and, Fate.

At this point it is important to note that while we have defined Fate as a force, this does not in any way preclude a theological approach to the analysis performed here. If Fate is a force, just as analogously gravity is a force, then just as the existence of a force of gravity does not preclude the existence of supernatural beings and intelligences, the existence of the force of Fate does not either. If indeed there are such beings as God and Satan and angels and demons, the manipulation of the forces of the world may very well be in their hands. It is also important to note that the transcendent part of the human being may very well be more readily related to such supernatural beings, which are also personalities, than it is to a blind force.

Given then that Fate is a force with which the human being must always contend, and that the human being is essentially free, how can one act in the face of Fate? Our final question.

First, however, we must make an observation: If Fate is a force, it is not an intelligence. Therefore, while we as human beings cannot meaningfully and usefully know the future, so much less so can a blind force. Indeed, given that the human being does possess an intellect, it would be that much easier for a human being to know the future and use the future. As a corollary, however, if Fate is manipulated by supernatural beings, one had better quickly pick a revealed religion, get right with God, and forget all of this philosophical nonsense!

Returning to the philosophical nonsense after our excursion into fair play, realizing that the future is essentially closed, it must be evident that the only place where Fate and the person meet in open contest is in the present moment. The present is the playing field of the game of life.

It is also in the present that freedom, which is the essence of the person, is exercised. Freedom is exercised in the present in the presence of the given. Following our earlier definition of the union of freedom and the given, we can define this union, which originally takes place in the present, as a work of art. But again we must recognize that not just any encounter of freedom and the given in the present constitutes creativity and thus a work of art. Freedom cannot blindly or unconsciously exist in the presence of the given, but must instead be imposed upon, or at least consciously united with the given to be called art. This follows from our earlier discussion of art, and especially the insights of Wittgenstein, in which a work of art is a work of art by virtue of its being lifted out of the everyday, unconscious passage of time and things, and, its recognition as a work of art; in other words, its presentation.

As odd as all of this may sound, there are examples of entire societies based upon this principle. In these societies even the most mundane activities are seen as art. Oscar Wilde delightfully argues that classical Greece was just such a society.[144] Pre-revolutionary Bourbon France is another. But a society in which everything from sweeping dirt to pouring tea to drawing a sword is a work of art, is Japan. We will return again to the Japanese example in our discussion of *Budo*, but for anyone who would doubt this assertion, I simply request that they go to a Japanese restaurant, order anything on the menu, and observe how it is served. The same, of course, can be said of classical French cuisine. Look around such places. Observe the service one is given. The etiquette, the dress, the decor. These are worlds in which the moment is intended as art.

Now we can answer our final question: "How should one act in the face of fate?" One should act consciously to unite one's freedom with the given — including one's fate — to create beauty.

Beauty, like nearly every other abstract term is, of course, almost indefinable. We find ourselves again in a Platonic quandary. We see many things in the world which we can call beautiful: paintings, sculptures, furniture, automobiles, individual men and women, and even actions, dance, athletic performances. The term can also be applied to moral actions. Self-sacrifice or a generous and loving gesture may be recognized as a beautiful act. All of these responses we accept as accurate or at least comprehensible and meaningful. If someone says to us, for example, "That was a beautiful gesture," we understand what they mean. However, like the problems confronting Plato, how do we recognize beauty in the many things and gestures of the world? How do we know what is beautiful? What, if anything, do all beautiful things and actions share to make them beautiful?

This is no coffee table chatter that we are discussing here. This is a central issue, not so much for art itself, but more importantly for the basis of morality and ethics. Art we have defined as freedom and the given united for a presentation. Art could thus be anything, in any medium, and does not have to be beautiful. Art can be quite strange, grating and ugly. Ethics, on the other hand, cannot. Ethics should never partake of the ugly. In this respect, positive law, that is law created and legislated by men and women for society, is more like art. Its end is order and it can be absolutely barbaric, negative, unfair, and unfeeling, and still be a union of freedom and the given in presentation to a human being and his or her society. Again, positive law and ethics are not the same thing.

But this answers none of our questions concerning ethics and beauty. And unfortunately we will not be attempting to answer them in this chapter on Fate. Instead, we will defer a further discussion of beauty until the next two chapters where we will confront the issue in the context of virtue and *budo*.

Returning to our topic of Fate, we have stated that lives based on art are not only possible, but have given examples of entire societies, most notably Japan, that embody this concept. Japan's social, aesthetic, and ethical culture, however, is derived from China.[145] It is to China, therefore, that we must look for an inclusion of Fate into the structures of everyday life and for clues on how to act in the face of Fate.

As we saw in the previous chapter, Confucianism eventually became the official philosophy of the Chinese Empire. It

was the basis not only for the regulation of morality and
social relations, but also for the official civil service examinations.[146] The philosophy of Confucius was spread throughout
East Asia wherever Chinese officials, merchants, or travelers
went.[147] It thus was imported into Japan, and its principles
were incorporated into Japanese life.[148]

Confucius and his followers in the Ju School adhered to
the Doctrine of the Mean, eschewing excess in any matter.[149]
This doctrine at once incorporated the principles of harmony, justice, and love. Also included in the Confucian outlook
was the root idea of doing one's very best for the sake of others.[150] These Confucian principles will be discussed further
in the next chapter, but suffice it to observe at this point that
these ideas — harmony, justice, and the dedication to doing
one's best for others, are readily apparent in the style and
spirit of Japanese life.[151]

At the basis of the Confucian outlook is what Confucius
termed "knowing *Ming*."[152] *Ming* or Fate[153] was defined by
Confucius as both the Decree of Heaven, which is closer to
our Western concept of Fate, and also, the "existent condition of the universe,"[154] or, as we have defined it, the given.
For Confucius, *Ming* or Fate was something inevitable and
independent of human efforts. It is the forces beyond our
control.[155] Confucius required that one recognize that many
things in the world are beyond one's control and subject to
Ming. Nonetheless, one must act. However, due to the pervasiveness of *Ming*, one must act without regard to success or
failure which were beyond one's control and in the realm of
Ming.[156] Acting in this manner and with this outlook was
"knowing *Ming*" for Confucius.[157]

Most importantly, it is from this knowledge that many, if
not most things are beyond one's control, that ethics is born.
Actually, for Confucius, it was *Jen*, or love which is born of
the knowledge of *Ming*, but *Jen* is a virtue and the basis of all
other virtues[158] as we shall see in the next chapter.
Nonetheless an important insight is embodied in this recognition of *Jen* as a reaction to *Ming* or Fate. It is because
human life is lived in the face of the Other, but especially
including Fate as that which humans cannot control, that

love and hate become possible at all. If the world were a totally solipsistic affair in which everything was under one's control and could be made to go exactly as one wanted it, the ideas of attraction and repulsion, love and hate, would be meaningless. Perhaps this is where energy comes in. Energy is the ability to do work. To perform a task. Action. Energy is produced by tension. Opposition creates tension. The more tension, the more energy is produced.[159] This energy is used to meet the opposition. *Ming* is the model of opposition. It is the ground of human being. Every encounter in the world mirrors or contains an element of *Ming*. Therefore, every encounter generates a degree of energy. The conscious channeling of this energy is what ethics is all about. We shall return to this matter.

The discussion in this chapter has gone from an average whiplash lawsuit through the metaphysical forces affecting human being and ended with energetics. But what does all this mean to us in our everyday life?

Again, the philosophical outlook of Confucius gives us guidance. Confucius was attempting to educate the rulers of the state.[160] His goal was to so cultivate the goodness and virtuousness in his students that when these students, who were not to retire from the world as those adhering to Taoism and Buddhism would, became public servants they would be so developed as virtuous men that they would make society, and thus human life, virtuous and good for all people.[161]

Eventually, as noted, the Confucian Classics became the basis for the civil service tests of the Chinese Empire. Unlike our own civil service where the emphasis is on "how to," but more like the Imperial British Civil Service, the Chinese Civil Service looked for "good people." The virtuous person was to administer the state.

The use of Confucian philosophy and learning as the basis of the civil service brings us back to everyday life. The people we are speaking of here are the nuts and bolts of Chinese Imperial society. They are not just the Emperor's court and entourage, but the magistrates and clerks who ran the day-to-day affairs down to the most minute and level of the organization — the Chinese Empire.

Many of us are involved in similar types of lives. We go to
college or business school, and enter a large organization —
a corporation or some level of government. As a prosecutor,
a state employee, I can testify that in the lives of all of us as
professionals, managers, or staff personal, *Ming* is a constant
force to be reckoned with. We are the types of people of
whom Confucius was thinking.

Managers and administrators are the first who come to
mind when thinking of the confrontation with *Ming*. Both
business and government exist in a world in which only a
small number of people are committed to their goals. An
example would be national health care. The President, his
wife, and a great number of his staff are pushing, pulling, tug-
ging, and bending at the time of this writing to create a system that would provide universal coverage in America.
There are thirty-nine million Americans who are not presently covered by health insurance and who would presumably
support these measures. However, there are approximately
two hundred fifty million people in the United States. The
insurance companies, and presumably their employees and
advisors, are opposed to universal coverage and health care
reform. Segments of the medical community, the specialists,
are also opposed. And a large percentage of the American
public is cautious or ambivalent. To proceed, the administrators, be they presidents or legal interns, are certainly smack
up against *Ming*. The attempt to control or simply to guide
these forces is gargantuan. How does one act in this environment, in this reality?

Just attempting to get a local county level landfill in place
— as the trash is overflowing day by day from the old one —
is daunting. Nobody wants it in their back yard. Yet the community, everyone, needs it. It must go somewhere. Plans are
drawn. Interest groups and neighborhood organizations
oppose it. New plans are drawn. The trash keeps overflowing. New organizations oppose it. An ambitious lawyer takes
the side of his neighborhood organization. He runs against
the mayor, putting political pressure on him. How does the
mayor, his city manager, his sanitation director, the environ-

mental engineers, act in the face of this brand of *Ming*?

Since the essence of business is, at least theoretically, competition, it is implied from the outset that business people will be face-to-face with *Ming* throughout their careers. Company A wants to sell widgets in a small, less developed nation. Company B gets the same idea. Business in this nation is a matter of strange rituals and dependent upon incomprehensible relationships. The government controls access, but authority to do so is spread out to a bewildering number of individuals in the most unlikely of positions. Bribery is a norm, almost like tipping. Will Company A play the game? If it does not, will Company B? Can either be assured that they are getting accurate information from their in-country advisors? Do the advisors have a covert agenda?

You are on Company A's team in this country. Welcome to the wonderful world of *Ming*.

You want to be the company controller. So does Fred. Fred golfs with the vice-president in charge of finance. But you have just received effusive compliments for a project you did for the retiring controller who is an old friend of the CEO. Factions are forming. Somebody in sales has a grudge with Fred and possibly some dirt from when Fred did sales. However, the head of marketing would like to move up and it is rumored that he and Fred are becoming friendly, and marketing has access to the CEO. The head of marketing could use the support of another senior executive, say the new controller, to further his own ideas. It goes on and on. Opposition is everywhere, and some careers have *Ming* built right in.

Lawyers in our adversarial system of law come immediately to mind, especially trial lawyers. Trial lawyers make an appointment with *Ming* every time they walk into a courtroom. The two lawyers can be brilliant; they can know the law and procedure inside out and backwards. They can play on it like virtuosos. Their witnesses can be coached to the point of Oscar nominations, but the ultimate decision does not belong to the lawyers. It belongs to twelve, usually less educated and knowledgeable citizens, who are empanelled as a jury. They are opaque, and are affectionately called "skulls" by practicing trial lawyers. Nobody knows what the skulls will do. You can work the hardest and do the best job you have ever done, and the skulls can turn against you. *Ming*.

Sales personnel also come to mind. Again, the ultimate decision is not the salesperson's. One can show the need for the product. One can show its usefulness, its appeal. One can even provide ready access to financing and still have the sale die.

Marketing is just as subject to the vicissitudes of fate as sales. Remember the Edsel? Remember the new Coca-Cola? Remember Screaming Yellow Zonkers? No? They are tucked safely away in the veils of *Ming*.

Finally, there is the endeavor that makes *Ming* the sine qua non of its existence: investing. In late 1972 who could have predicted the Arab Oil Embargo? The stock market halved in value. As late as August, 1929, the established economists were calling for more of the boom in the market.

During the third week of October, 1987, I was working as a branch counsel for a land title company. I had been sent to Richmond, Virginia for advanced training. About the second afternoon of the session, our trainer, a corporate vice-president, entered the room with the palest complexion this side of the grave to announce that he was not able to teach that day, and that classes would be cancelled and that he would meet us all at the company-sponsored dinner that evening. The market had fallen two hundred points the previous day and was down another five hundred that morning.

That evening martinis and Manhattans flowed in rivers. I, always the realist, ate the most expensive items on the menu, complete with cocktails, liqueur, imported beers, desert, coffee, after-dinner liqueurs, and a cigar. Dinner was on Mr. *Ming*.

There never has been a consistent, totally reliable way in which to invest. In fact, as anyone who follows *Wall Street Week* knows, there are creatures in the investment world that host Louis Rukeyser calls "elves." These "elves" are actually "technical analysts." Now this term "technical analyst" sounds wonderfully scientific. Why then does Mr.

Rukeyser call them "elves"? It is because technical analysts make predictions on the performance of the stock market by drawing up elaborate charts of the performances not of the companies the stocks represent, not of the trends or history of various industries, not of sales, financial positions, or production. No, the elves draw charts showing the ups and downs of the stocks themselves, completely removed from any association with the economy or the world outside of the stocks themselves! All of the rest of this data, termed fundamentals, is irrelevant. How far this is removed from the cycles of the planets is known only to a few hermits deep in the Himalayas.

Recognizing then that Fate or *Ming* so deeply affects our lives and nowhere more so than in our professional lives, one begins to gain an appreciation for Confucius' insight, and to recognize that he was thinking of people just such as these when he made his philosophical pronouncements for the Chinese civil servants. Modern managers, professionals, marketers, sales people, and money managers hold positions in many ways similar to the bureaucrats whom Confucius envisioned. The professional lives of all of these groups involve the accomplishment or goals, hopefully for the good of all but certainly for the organization and, in all of these positions, people are dependent upon the decisions and actions of the manager, professional, or public official. Confucius reminds us all that we must first recognize our limits. We are all subject to Fate.

How then shall we act in the face of *Ming*? A clue is given by Confucius' admonition to act without regard to success or failure. He does not say this so that human beings, and certainly those human beings who have the lives and well being of others in their hands, should be paralyzed and fail to act. Instead, his advice is to show that there is no path that one can choose that one can control. We can neither see nor control the future. Realizing that, but still having responsibility for the lives or finances of others, even the most pragmatic of businesspeople needs a rudder, a guide. Confucius provides this by arguing that the realization that so much is subject to fate frees the human being. How? It allows one to act any way one wishes. It allows one to act against selfish interests. It allows one to create, to unite freedom with the given, to present oneself. The human being is free to act ethically.

As we have stated, ethical behavior is a form of art. It, like art, is the combination of freedom and the given in the present to make a presentation. Ethical acts, however, also have the requirement that they be aesthetically pleasing. Beautiful in themselves. Creation requires energy, and this energy is produced by the constant opposition between individual freedom and "thing." The build-up of this energy and its present, conscious diversion towards beauty is called virtue. Not virtue in the sense a prissy, church lady in Kalamazoo, but in the old Roman sense of strength. In this sense, ethics is a form of *Qi Gong*, the Chinese discipline of energy control. While *Qi Gong* was developed primarily by Taoists,[162] as time went on Confucian ideas crept into Taoism and vice versa. There are several types of *Qi Gong*, one of which is called "scholarly" or *Ju Qi Gong*[163] which was used by the Chinese scholars — magistrates — to clear the mind and give them the strength and vision to perform their duties (a low-level Chinese magistrate governed as many as two hundred and fifty thousand people) in an ethical manner. Further, as a survival method, *Qi Gong*, by building physical and mental strength and stability, kept the harried magistrates from the heart attacks, strokes, and physical problems that accompany the stress of management.

Confucius argued that given the fact that we are subject to fate, the only reasonable course is to act virtuously. One can worry endlessly as to the practicality and success of any course of action — will the new ad campaign work? Was taking an option on wheat futures a good idea? But one can always sleep when one has acted virtuously. The resolution of opposing forces is almost a physical relief or high.

In the next chapter we will examine virtue. We will see it in terms of its nature as strength and in terms of its energetic content. In many ways the feeling of acting virtuously resembles the pleasant feeling one gets after a good and productive workout.

Confucius was, after all, possibly the first to say that virtue is its own reward.[164]

CHAPTER THREE

Virtue: Its Bioenergetics and Sexuality

In the winter of 1966 I was a humble student at a humble junior college in Pennsylvania. York Junior College was a school for kids who screwed-off in high school but decided sometime during the summer after graduation that college beat work. It was also a repository for all of the idiot nephews and nieces who coasted through prep school and had nowhere else to go, since real colleges still had standards at that time. It was the kind of place where the janitor forbade students from using red or blue light bulbs in their rooms since it was his theory that colored light bulbs used a different type of electricity. It was the kind of place where the college president backed him up. It was the kind of place that thrived because of the Vietnam War.

In central Pennsylvania in 1966 there was only beginning to be an opposition to the war. Being an institution of higher learning, dedicated to the free and open debate of issues of concern, my junior college decided to have a public discussion of the war. In a spirit of fair play, nobody opposing the war was invited to speak. The only speaker was a rotund, poorly-dressed, and appallingly ignorant, right-wing radio "personality." Things never change, do they?

Strangely, even at a party school like my junior college, the place was packed. The Personality launched forth with a jingoistically-oriented analysis of the situation in Southeast Asia that was so stupid and inept that a real jingoist would have slapped him in his face. I, being the humble, shy, and retiring person I was, endured most of this nonsense until he began to get his historical facts wrong. Over the years I've grown accustomed to this from other radio "personalties," and even presidents of the United States, but at that time I was a callow youth — and a history major — and I couldn't stand it.

I found myself on my feet. An argument ensued. I educated my right-wing friend on the Geneva accords. I told him Geneva was in Switzerland. This seemed to puzzle him. When I sat down, the free and open discussion in an institution of higher learning was over.

Suddenly, as people left the hall, I was set upon by a group of coeds who previously didn't even deign to sneer at me (Humphrey Bogart's line to Peter Lorre in Casablanca came frequently to mind, "If I thought about you at all, I'd probably despise you")

At any rate, suddenly I was an interesting and popular person. Then, one of these lovely, and of course, intelligent, perceptive women informed me that a group of jocks was waiting outside to beat the tar out of me. This was 1966, after all. She was even so kind as to point out the door I should avoid.

Now, I weighed this matter in my mind. I was suddenly popular with women on my campus because I spoke my mind. And all I had to do was die for it! It seemed like a fair deal to me at the time, being eighteen with a brain submerged in hormones.

After making funeral arrangements, I made it a point to exit through the door I had been warned away from. Nobody was there. It was cold, and so was the beer that night. This was a junior college and there were priorities. Beer versus political commitment. My assailants chose beer. I love this country.

I am not a brave person, let me be the first in a potentially long line of people to tell you, but on that winter night nearly thirty years ago, I couldn't stop myself. That windbag was just plain wrong. He was distorting the truth and acting from God-knows-what motives. When it was over and I was being warned — and in those days people were beaten for speaking their mind — I chose to face the threat head-on. I'm basically a coward, but it was easy to be, or at least to act, brave that evening because I felt that I was morally right. Also, there were women to impress.

The dictionary definition of "virtue" indicates that the term is derived from the Latin word vir or man. Virtue means, among other things, "manliness."[165] I like to think of it as strength. When a person fails morally, we say they are weak. When we tell someone to resist evil or temptation, we tell them to be strong. Virtue, strength, is the essence, the sine qua non of ethical behavior. Since ethical behavior many times requires that we act against our own interests, strength is necessary to resist and stand firm against the consequences of the ethical act.

Standing firm is the root of ethics. As we have seen in our discussion of the human being and of Confucianism, the human being exists in a world in which he or she is constantly contending with *Ming*, or fate. He or she cannot predict or control the vicissitudes of *Ming*. Recognition of this fact is the beginning of ethics, according to Confucianism.[166]

I stated earlier that the term "virtue" comes from the Latin term *vir* meaning "man" or "manly." Cassall's *New Compact Latin Dictionary* adds to this definition "a man of character or courage," "he-man," and also, "a soldier, especially an infantryman." Curiously, while *vir* is a masculine noun, *virtus* is feminine but still means "manliness, excellence, worth, goodness, virtue, bravery, courage."[167]

Now the actual Latin word for strength, power, or force is *vis*, which is also a feminine noun. Its plural, however, is *vires,* and in the plural it, like *vir,* has a military meaning as in "troops, forces."[168] It seems, therefore, that the terms *vir* and *vis* are related.

I don't want to tax anyone's patience (which, by the way, is also a virtue), but the Greek word for virtue, ἀρετή ,also means manliness. Strangely, a second definition is also given for virtue in Greek, that is ἐνέργεια, or energy. Now this association of energy with virtue is simply a synonym, but this synonymous definition occurs in English. One of the definitions given for virtue in the *Oxford English Dictionary, 2d Edition,* is "power, energy."

This is fascinating since it gives virtue an active character. Virtue is not some *thing*, some law chipped on a stone tablet, but is a process, a by-product of energy and the power represented and unleashed by energy. We will discuss energy more fully below, but suffice it to say at this point that virtue, although a feminine term, denotes masculine characteristics, and is active, associated with power and energy.

From where, however, does this power and energy come? Again, clues are given from classical word derivations and usages. ἀρετή, as was stated, is the Greek term for virtue. It also indicates manliness. As used in the *New Testament*, however, ἀρετή, indicates something interior.[169] It is a power or energy coming from inside. Is this usage by the church fathers legitimate?

We spoke earlier of the relationship of the roots *vir*, man, and *vis*, force, power, strength. This relationship is further developed and its implications displayed in the words that are formed from these roots. From *vir* are derived such words as virile and virility, which obviously describe masculinity, but also words such as *virago,* which is the Latin term for a female warrior, and virgin, or in Latin, *virgo*, which means maiden or girl. Both, of course, are feminine.

From *vis* comes the term viscus and viscera which mean flesh, meat, entrails, internal organs, and the heart or innermost part of anything.

Because of the association of *vir* and *vis*, we can see that the conjoining of manliness, strength, power, and energy with the interior, the heart or innermost part is indeed legitimate. Virtue is, as the translation of the *New Testament* presented it, an interior strength, power, or form of energy.

But what type of power or energy are we talking about? What is its nature? Clues again come from the ancient terms. Isn't it curious that terms such as virile and virgin come from the same root, *vir* or man? In English there are sexual connotations for both terms. Virility is associated with masculine sexual potential. Potency. Virginity, on the other hand, indicates a lack of sexual intercourse. While the term is applied most often to women or girls, it is also applied to men or boys who have not had intercourse. In English, when someone is inexperienced at something, we also say that they are "green." "Greenness" in the sense of youth and fresh life, or biological potential, is, not surprisingly, derived from the words formed from *vir. Viridan* means "green." *Vireo* means to be green, to be vigorous or healthy. *Virictum* means turf. *Viresco* to grow green. *Virga* is a green twig, a slip (a mere slip of a girl), a rod, or a wand. *Virgula* a little twig, staff, or rod. *Viridis* equals fresh, young, or vigorous. And *viriditas* equals freshness, greenness, or bloom. Finally, *viridarium* is a pleasure garden.

There are, accordingly, *biological* and, specifically, *sexual* connotations to the words formed from *vir.* The association with greenness in this case then is used in its sense as freshness, ripeness, potency. Of course, all of us who live in this post-Freudian era know quite clearly the psychic associations of "rods, sticks, boughs, and wands." They are symbols of male sexual potency.[170] This is further underscored by the formation of words indicating flesh and internal organs from the associated root *vis* and from the word *viscum,* meaning mistletoe. Why would the association with mistletoe be so revealing? Because the plant mistletoe was used by the ancient pagans as a symbol of the male genitalia. Its white berries were associated with sperm.[171] Finally, according to Jung, green is the color associated with physical sensation and sensuality.[172]

We see then the specifically male, biological and sexual roots of the concept of virtue. Virtue is an internal force or power which is basically biological and sexual in nature, and appears most naturally in the form of potency or potential energy.

Since the term virtue connotes sexual energy or potency, what are we to make of the fact that while it describes masculine attributes, it is a feminine noun? In fact, while *vir* is masculine, *vis* is feminine and most of the terms formed from both roots are feminine and to a lesser extent, neuter. Even the unquestionably masculine term *virilitas,* meaning manhood and virility, is a feminine noun!

A truth of bioenergetics seems to be involved here. Although we will explore this notion later on, bioenergy, specifically bioenergy that is associated with sexuality, has two aspects that are not separated except conceptually. *Qi*, the Chinese bioenergy, has two aspects — yin and yang. Yin is feminine and passive while yang is masculine and active. Yin and yang are constantly going through cycles, changing and transforming into one another.[173] Wilhelm Reich's orgone, of which I have written elsewhere, is a monopolar energy which is expressed in both male and female sexuality.[174] The recognition of this transmutability of sexual bioenergy is what appears to be at the basis of the gender assignments of the words derived from *vir* and *vis*.

Virtue then is power, energy in its aspect as potential and as potency. As such, it is the source of action. This is how it was viewed by the church fathers following St. Augustine.[175] Augustine associated virtue with the will.[176] Aquinas, too, although using the word *habitus* or habit with virtue, used *habitus* in the sense of concentrated and powerful willing.[177].

We have seen this type of will before in Schopenhauer. In Schopenhauer, however, the will is a blind, internal force striving only to preserve and expand its own existence.[178] Nietzsche took this will further and made of it a blind, irrational "will to power."[179] In other words, power is exercised solely for the sake of expanding or creating more power.[180]

Creation is, of course, another aspect of potential power and energy. Nietzche's "will to power" can destroy — witness the Nazis — but it also can create — witness the Code Napoleon, the music of Wagner, the architectural grandeur of imperial Rome. Creation and creativity also have sexual connotations, and the sublimation of sexual energy in order that it may be redirected into artistic and cultural expression has been thoroughly explored by Freud.[181]

Recalling the positions of the Nineteenth Century aesthetic philosophers, Hegel, Marx, Schopenhauer, and Nietzsche, we see that the human being is intrinsically, by virtue of his or her nature, a creator. The human being is human by virtue of his or her creativity. The human being possesses bio-sexual energy, which, as discovered by Nietzsche, Schopenhauer, and especially Marx, demands expression. Indeed Augustine calls virtue the art of living and, in Italian, *virtu* means "art."

▶ ▶

A human being is an artist or is not human. And a human is an artist only if he or she has virtue. All human beings have virtue to a greater or lesser degree. Therefore, as the Chinese philosophers following Mencius asserted, the original nature of human beings is good.

But what do we mean by "good"? Nietzsche was the first to explore this term in the context of biology in his writings *On the Genealogy of Morals* and *Beyond Good and Evil.*

In these works, Nietzsche argues that there is a distinction between "good" and "bad," and, "good" and "evil." This distinction is based on one's class perspective. "Good" and "bad" are distinctions made by aristocrats and those belonging to aristocratic cultures such, as Nietzsche asserts, as that of the ancient Greeks.[182] For those in the elite class of an aristocratic culture, "good" means themselves; the rich, healthy, beautiful, strong, and socially favored. "Bad," means the weak, sick, poor, and socially despised. Accordingly, the "good" of such a society is health, wealth, beauty, strength, and honor. To lose these is to become inferior or "bad."

In such a culture it is not even possible to use good and evil as opposites since there is no concept of "evil." We, as with our aristocratic forbearers, can easily recognize that it is not "evil" to be poor, weak, or sick. But, according to Nietzsche, due to our Judeo-Christian history, we may not so readily comprehend that it is likewise not "evil" to be rich, healthy, beautiful, and exalted in this world.[183] Christianity teaches that "The last shall be first and the first shall be last." Following in this tradition, the *Qur'an* also asserts that neither one's wealth or social position will avail one before Allah. Those who suffer will be rewarded. Accordingly, evil could be easily associated with the rich and powerful since they "love this world too much."[184]

Not so with the aristocratic cultures. To be rich and favored was good. Everything else was simply bad. There were no further moral overtones.

One can readily observe this attitude in the conduct of the Greek gods. They eat, drink, sleep around, and fight. Zeus' various and assorted rapes have the moral content of a fraternity prank. How can they act like this and not be excoriated? Because they are gods. They are favored. This is how they are expected to act.

Pre-revolutionary Bourbon France, which Nietzsche views approvingly, also possessed this attitude. The "divine right of kings" was invoked to justify all of the excesses, and, Nietzsche would add, all of the beauty from sculptured gardens to haute cuisine.

"L'Etat Ce Moi" ("the state is me") was enunciated with a clear conscience by Louis XIV. It was the type of society in which a French noble could run a child over with his carriage and inquire as to the injuries to his horses.[185]

That these class-specific divisions survive is indicated in such aristocratically inspired terms as "bourgeois" which means basically "middle class," and is a derogatory term.

When the vast majority of humankind, the poor, weak, sick, and underprivileged began, however, to assign terms, they saw things differently. One has only to read the *Beatitudes* in the *Sermon on the Mount* to understand the social and philosophical difference. "Blessed are the poor." "Blessed are the weak in spirit." "Blessed are those who hunger and thirst for justice. Theirs shall be the kingdom of Heaven." Also, "I tell you it shall be easier for a camel to pass through the eye of a needle than for a rich man to enter the Kingdom of Heaven."

It is also to be remembered that Jesus, besides preaching such revolutionary ideas, actually did some pretty outrageous acts — such as healing the sick, over the vociferous opposition of the Jewish priestly class. After all, in these ancient societies, the sick were "bad."

Thinkers and activists such as the Jewish prophets, Jesus, the Buddha, and Mohammed slowly changed the ancient system of values. The concept of "evil" was introduced and opposed to the term "good." This could be done since a new world, one ruled by a moral, or at least a just God, was posited. The Greek gods were certainly not moral and rarely, if ever, just, or, even at a minimum, fair. Just like the nobility here on earth. The new God, however, was fair and just, if nothing else, and his kingdom was reserved for the just; those who tried to be fair and "righteous." The good was still the "favored," but now it was the favored of God, and its assessment was to be performed in the new kingdom beyond this world. To be rich and favored in this world then meant nothing. To be poor and despised likewise meant nothing. God was just; so to be unjust, as the nobility frequently was, was to be "evil."

Nietzsche goes further, however, and begins to rant about the "herd" and "slave morality."[186] He argues that once the vast majority of humanity, the chronically underprivileged and abused felt their power, they indiscriminately assigned the term "evil" to all of the former aristocratic values. Therefore, wealth, health, beauty, and social standing became synonymous with evil. The rich and powerful, and, later, the talented, in fact, anyone who stood out from the crowd, were viewed per se as evil.

I stated that Nietzsche was the first to attempt some sort of biological interpretation of morality because he used the derivation and usage of the terms "good," "bad," and "evil" to show that the first connotation of these words was based on what would later be called "natural selection." Nature, biology, favored certain individuals and they, and the physical characteristics associated with them, were called "good." Unfortunately, however, Nietzsche was insufficiently biological, and, while a philologist, did not apparently pick up on the sexual and biophysical implications of the terms of the languages he studied. Nietzsche, in spite of all of his cant about a transvaluation of values, et cetera, was after all, a middle-class German professor of the Nineteenth Century. By focusing on only one group of human beings, the aristocratic, Nietzsche failed to recognize that all human beings possess the same biology and, accordingly, the same bioenergy. What does this truism mean, however? Does it invalidate Nietzsche's insight into human development and the creation of a new morality for a new type of super-human being?

As will be demonstrated in the discussion of bioenergetics and the Chinese practice and philosophy of *Qi Gong*, bioenergy is free, unlimited and all-pervasive. Therefore, by the skilled use of this energy, cures can be effected, potentialities and talents developed, and the human being, nearly any human being, improved. Any human being can work to overcome and surpass him or herself. This is precisely what Nietzsche hoped for in his doctrine of the Superman.[187] Must we, as with Nietzsche, simply allow nature to blindly select a few fortunate individuals by chance, as with the aristocratic societies of old, or, can we enter into a partnership with nature in such a way as to develop the natural energy that we all possess? In other words, in answer to the old Greek question, "Can virtue be taught?," we can answer yes. But not in the form in which it has traditionally been conceived. As in *Qi Gong*, and certain forms of psychotherapy, a person can be taught not what is good, bad, or evil, but rather how to develop one's bioenergy; one's inherent virtue. Goodness, health, wealth, beauty, self-respect, and self-expression flow from this.

What becomes of Nietzsche's aristocratic culture once the implications of virtue are recognized and applied? It becomes irrelevant. This is the basic insight of Karl Marx. All men and woman are capable and have the ability, the virtue for self-respect and self-expression. All of us are capable of expressing our basically good human nature as artists.

In his earliest book, *The Birth of Tragedy from the Spirit of Music*, Nietzsche outlined the response of the Greek people to the capriciousness of human life. In other words, the Greek response to the power of Fate, or, in our present discussion, *Ming*. According to Nietzsche, this response came in two forms: the Apollonian, which dealt in dreams and the plastic arts; and, the Dionysian, which was associated with intoxication and music. As with Schopenhauer, these were the sources of art, and art was an escape from the demands of the Will, a way to ward off the Fates, if just briefly. As a classicist, Nietzsche should have been aware of the fact that ἀρετή, or virtue, in her personification as a goddess (not as a human being, as in the story of the Argonauts) was reputed to be the *daughter of Dionysius*, and the teacher of justice to Hercules.[188] Again, the Confucian insight of virtue growing from the confrontation with Fate or *Ming* is demonstrated. Nietzsche's failing is that, while he excoriated others for their passivity, he himself stops at the Dionysian drunkenness in the face of fate. This very intoxication is a blatant indication of the passive acceptance of fate. Of impotence. While Nietzsche praises the superman, his superman is randomly selected by fate or nature. Nature is never questioned, and this lack of inquiry leads to ignorance.

Can virtue be taught? Yes. That education is the key to virtue or knowledge is the basic insight of Jesus, Buddha, Plato — and Confucius. Socrates says "know thyself." The gospels assert "The truth shall make you free." And, "Do ye not know that ye are as gods?" Perhaps Nietzsche's fault, and this is a fault of many insular Euro-centric scholars, is the limitation of his researches to Western classical sources. In China, due to its Confucian and Taoist background, he would have found a society that transcended the aristocratic, permitting, through its bureaucratic examination system, individual merit to be truly recognized. This is because both the Taoist and Confucian philosophers place the highest and most central emphasis on self-cultivation. This is an exceedingly democratic ideal and is that much more ancient than the aristocratic as China is to Greece.

If Schopenhauer and Nietzsche's developments of the insight that the human being is composed in part of an unconscious, blind will or power that has its roots in the pre-rational, instinctual world of nature are flawed, the insights themselves stood and were productively utilized not so much by academic philosophy, but by the depth psychologists who first presented their theories and models of the human psyche at the end of the Nineteenth Century. The first of these, of course, was Sigmund Freud.*

Freud did not single-handedly create all of the elements of depth psychology, but he did bring many diverse observations and theoretical constructs together in one unified model of the total human being and his or her behavior. While experimental behavioral psychologists, such as Wundt and Watson, puttered around in their laboratories focusing on snippets of human and animal behavior, Freud, originally

---

* For the following discussion on Freud, Jung, Reich, depth psychology, and Chinese Qi Gong, I refer the reader to my previous book, The Tao of Bioenergetics, YMAA Publications Center (1993). The chapters referring to these matters are extensively footnoted and more fully developed than space permits here.

also a medical researcher, developed his theories from clinical observation of real and total human beings who were still firmly ensconced in a real world outside of the laboratory.

Practicing psychiatrists and neurologists during the Nineteenth Century were confounded with the problem of "hysteria." While the hysterical patient was unable to function in society, and often displayed physical symptoms, there was no underlying somatic basis for these physical manifestations. To a medical culture that had, due to the advances in bacteriology, inoculation, drug research, and internal surgery, become completely materialistic during the second half of the century, hysterical patients were maddening — for the physicians. According to materialistic theory, they were either considered malingerers or pronounced incurable.

Freud, as a neurologist, became interested in this problem. From an older colleague, a Dr. Josef Breuer, Freud heard of at least one successful cure. Breuer had used hypnosis to get one of his hysterical patients to talk about her illness. As a result of simply "talking," the patient improved and was considered "cured." Freud went to France and studied hypnosis under Charcot and Bernheim. His eventual collaboration with Breuer produced the first book of depth psychology in 1895, *Studies In Hysteria*.

Freud was a lousy hypnotist and eventually dropped any pretence of it in his practice. Instead, he simply let his patients talk. He also began to explore their dreams, propounding a theory of dream analysis in his work, *The Interpretation of Dreams*. According to Freud, dreams were not the result of indigestion or a mental rehash of the day's proceedings, but a different language from a different level of the total person. Dreams spoke in symbols of things that the conscious, Victorian mind would not dare entertain. Mostly, according to Freud, this level of the mind spoke about sex,[189] the most taboo of Victorian subjects.

What, however, did all of this mean to the clinical picture of the real human being with whom Freud dealt? It meant quite clearly that human beings were not simply one dimensional, stimulus-response machines, nor were they some sort of electro-chemical apparatus such as the tubes and beakers in a laboratory. The human being had levels, depth.

Freud, being the outstanding researcher that he was, needed to develop a theoretical framework in which to fit his clinical observations. How could a single human being speak two different psychic languages? From where were the symbolic insights and observations manifested in dreams coming? Why couldn't these insights be made consciously? Why was there the need at all for a "symbolic" language such as that displayed in dreams?

Beginning with the reason for the two languages, Freud concluded that since the Victorian society in which he practiced could not accept certain ideas and behavior, and went so far as to physically punish even simple curiosity about certain physical, especially sexual, bodily functions and relationships, the mind needed some avenue to express this fascinating material. Because a person would be punished for expressing these subjects publicly or consciously, they were submerged, "repressed," and passed below the level of consciousness, but did not disappear. Instead, they were expressed only in the most private level of mental activity — the dream. Even in the dream, however, these taboo contents could not be expressed "rationally," that is, discursively as in everyday conscious conversation. Instead, they were displayed in symbols which could fool the inhibiting censors of the conscious mind. In order, therefore, to get to what was causing a patient's behavioral and mental problems, Freud would "read" and interpret the symbolic conversations of his patient's dreams.

This procedure and these observations raise several questions, the most important of which are: First, from where are these symbolic statements coming, and, secondly, what is the mechanism that makes it work?

Concerning the question of from where these symbols come, we return to the insights of Schopenhauer and Nietzsche concerning a blind, unconscious will. Freud initially divided the human mind, for theoretical purposes, into a conscious and an unconscious. The conscious mind, of course, is our everyday "rational" interactions with ourselves, other people, and our environment. Its thoughts are practical and make an effort at being adaptive to its world. The unconscious contains those elements that are not acceptable to the conscious mind. They represent impractical, self-centered, infantile responses and orientations that the conscious mind determines are self-defeating and unadaptive to the external world.

Eventually Freud expanded this model into three parts: The id, ego, and superego. The id was the deepest, instinctual, and most primitive part of the mind. It was completely subjective and demanded instant gratification of its very pressing biological needs. It operated on what Freud terms the "pleasure principle." The superego, on the other hand, was the repository of all of one's childhood moral training. The imperative, the "Thou shalt not," et cetera. Both the id and the superego were considered to be removed from reality in that their commands and demands were to be met whether or not they were appropriate to the conditions in the real world. The id would like sex in the punch bowl at a cocktail party; and the superego would have you starve rather than steal a loaf of bread.

It was only the ego that dealt in the real word with what Freud termed "the reality principle." The ego had to at once satisfy the real pressures and stimuli of the real, conscious world, and the demands of both the id and the superego. If the ego could not fulfill this balancing act, irrational behavior developed along with neurosis or even psychosis.

Freud's model of the mind is definitely a workable hypothesis, and can, if not taken too rigidly or too ontologically concretely, give a practitioner an idea of from where mental attitudes and symptoms come. It admirably asserts the fact that human actions are not always a simple, conscious response to stimuli, but are composites of different motivations and assumptions, and, that the human being has different levels; he or she has depths. However, as satisfying as this model is, the question remains, how does it work?

In his own work, and, in my book, *The Tao of Bioenergetics*, the mechanics of Freud's model of the mind are found to be dependent on a theory of psychic energy, or, what Freud called "libido."

Looking at Freud's model of the mind, it is easy to make the three divisions, id, ego, and superego into "things," or, actual "places." In other words, the tendency is to view something like the id, a theoretical construct, as something like the stomach or the liver; a specific thing located in a specific place. However, this was not how Freud viewed human psychology.

Freud understood that he could never explain how an item that was "unconscious," and therefore, unknown by definition, could ever become "conscious." How could it cross the line? This is where the theory of psychic energy or "libido" came in.

Similarly to Kant and to the Hindu and Buddhist philosophies of perception, the mind is active. It actively reaches out into the world to "grab" objects. Like Buddhist perceptual theory, it does not simply and indiscriminately mirror everything in the perceptual field, but is attracted to items that are important to it, items which are significant enough to irritate the mind, items which produce and draw energy. Obviously, the more energy in a psychic content — and that is what any perceptual item becomes once grasped by the mind — the more likely it is to thrust itself into the conscious field. Likewise, ideas that are repressed and pushed below the line of consciousness do not simply disintegrate, but if significant enough, continue to draw energy while in the unconscious. Dreams then are "pictures" of energy. Psychic constructs that attract enough energy can even intrude on waking consciousness in the form of irrational behavior, defense mechanisms such as rationalizations, and, in the so-called "Freudian slips" of speech. None of this is possible without the mechanism of psychic energy which allows psychic contents to be "mobile" or dynamic. Indeed, any theory of dynamic psychology, as envisioned by Freud, would be impossible without a theory of psychic energy.

In answer as to how this psychic energy was produced, Freud argued that it came from the instincts —sex, hunger, survival, et cetera; that is, libido came from the physical organism, from biology. To the end of his life, Freud, the neurologist, believed that a physical basis for libido would and could eventually be found.

Sigmund Freud's younger colleague and heir apparent was the Swiss psychologist, Carl Jung. Before encountering Freud, Jung was a brilliant clinical psychiatrist in his own right, beginning his practice at the Burgholzli Mental Hospital in 1900. Jung's original work was in *dementia praecox*, or schizophrenia. He found Freud's work, although not accepted by the established medical community, to be the most practical and theoretically sound of all the medical literature dealing with mental pathology.

Although Jung is most closely identified with his work on symbology, mythology, and what he termed the "collective unconscious," he, like Freud, developed the theory of psychic energy to demonstrate a theoretical mechanism for his own depth psychology. Jung published his theories in a short book entitled *On Psychic Energy*.

At the outset, while acknowledging that psychic energy probably is, in fact, biological in nature, Jung arbitrarily limits his study to purely "psychic" as opposed to somatic energy. He also sees this energy as belonging to a "closed" system. In fairness, he admits that this procedure is arbitrary and is only used for purposes of explication.

Jung, like Freud, posits a dynamic personality. This implies that the human personality is always in a state of flux; always changing. Like Freud, Jung argues that change is impossible without a theory of energy which is the vehicle of psychic changes as much as energy is the vehicle of changes in physics.

From a medical point of view, the human personality needs to develop. Accordingly, Jung developed a theory of the "stages of life." The personality must progress and mature in order to find completion in the world. I use the term "completion." Jung, however, referred to this process as "individuation." That is, the process by which the human being becomes a whole and balanced individual as opposed to a psychically fragmented "mass man." The problem of a lack of psychic integration, of course, is that since the various "parts" of the personality are unconnected and do not communicate with each other, unrealistic and inappropriate responses to the diverse stimuli of the world can and do occur. The personality is thus buffeted by the world and exists in a purely "reactive" mode, having no creative control over its own life. Since, as we have seen, creativity is the essence of humanity, such a person is living a less than human life.

For Jung, as for Freud, psychic contents attract and produce energy. This energy, for Jung, is channeled through what he terms "gradients." Energy flows from areas of higher potential to those of lower. It is purely a quantitative matter. As psychic contents "connect," "constellations," that is, spider webs of related (not necessarily rationally, but rather energetically) contents are formed. As with Freud, Jung believed in the principle of conservation of energy. In other words, the quantity of psychic energy is fixed. It cannot be created or destroyed. Therefore, as a quantity of energy is depleted in one area of the psyche, it must appear in equal quantity somewhere else.

Interestingly, Jung tackled the problem of symbols head on. Since the symbols used in dreams recurred from patient to patient, Jung believed that there was something more universal to humankind involved. His studies of mythology led him to believe in a repertoire of symbols common to all humankind, and that these universal symbols are the products of a very deep, creative portion of the mind which Jung termed the "collective unconscious." The collective unconscious, like the physical body, possessed "organs" and channels and spoke *objectively* to the mind, very much as physical, external reality did, in an effort to push the organism to a more creative and adaptive balance. The symbols, unlike under Freud's theory, are not used to disguise unacceptable personal fixations, but exist in their own right and act as energy directors, valves so to speak. They attract and distribute energy for the dynamic purposes of development. For Jung, by using these symbols, energy can be directed so that higher, more complete states of integration and balance can be achieved, uniting the psyche so that maximum adaptation and self-expression can be achieved. Unlike Freud, who dealt in pathology, adaptation in the sense of being comfortably able to fit into one's environment, was not the end all and be all. Adaptation for Jung was a pre-requisite, only a basis that could make one's *creativity possible.*

As was stated, both Freud and Jung saw psychic energy in terms similar to physical energy. This energy could neither be produced nor destroyed. Therefore, its quantity could neither be decreased nor increased. Further, both men, while acknowledging the undoubted physical or biological source of this energy, failed to seriously pursue the matter further. Both were clinicians whose practical medical concerns made them arbitrarily draw a line around the psyche and make it a "closed system."

This procedure, however, was totally unsatisfying to Freud's youngest, and possibly most brilliant student — Wilhelm Reich.

Reich came from a family steeped in personal tragedy. Both his mother and father committed suicide after the mother was caught in an extramarital affair. Wilhelm Reich at age seventeen was left to manage a large farm in the Ukraine. He left the farm during World War I and became an officer in the Austrian Army. After the war, Reich began his medical studies in Vienna. He became the head of a Freudian study group, was accepted by Freud as a clinical assistant, and was entrusted by Freud, while in his twenties, with the leadership of Freud's Seminar for Psychoanalytic Therapy. In this capacity he was in charge of the ongoing training of much older and more established analysts.

Probably as a result of his personal tragedy, Reich's medical interests concentrated on sexuality. Reich wanted to find the biological or physical basis of Freud's work, especially his theory of libido.

Unlike Jung, Reich held the position that libido was basically sexual in nature. Following from this vitalistic point of view, Reich also began to view the total human being in "functional" terms, that is, in terms of what is *done* or accomplished by this sexual energy, not simply in terms of rigid physical or mental "structures." Additionally, Reich viewed sexual energy as functioning in the entire body as opposed simply to the gonads.

In his first revision of Freudian theory, Reich argued that the release of tension during the sexual act was not the goal of the instincts. Instead, the instincts were *active* and involved in reaching out to the world. The instincts for Reich *actively sought pleasure.* This distinction is crucial since it contrasts with Freud's negative, more passive adaption to conditions as they are in society, complete with its varying degrees of repression. Reich's instincts were active and seeking something more fulfilling than mere adaptation. Reich also associated pleasure with the activity of the muscles themselves rather than simply being the result of muscular activity. Free muscular movement was essential to the unrestricted pursuit of pleasure, which was the deep-seated goal of human instincts.

Now this is again similar to the will of Schopenhauer and Nietzsche, and, to the Id of Freud. However, there is one crucial difference. Those prior thinkers all viewed the instincts or the will with suspicion. The instincts or the will could provide the energy for great works of art and culture, but could just as easily and just as frequently lead to great destruction either individually or socially. Reich's view of the instincts was totally positive. Very much like the Chinese Taoists, Reich believed that when not prevented by outside forces, the pleasure principle would only lead to a self-regulated and trusting person who was capable of naturally and gracefully expressing him or herself. The sex act, the genuine, uninhibited, and unperverted sex act with its physical movement, surrender, and trust was the model of this self-expression. Reich believed that the instincts could and should be trusted.

Clinically, Reich began to notice that his patients were not as forthcoming about their problems in their dream material as Freud had theorized. He was dismayed that analysis was taking longer and longer and now beginning to stretch into years on the couch — many times with no "cure." Reich began to notice, however, that nearly all of his patients had tight and restrictive muscular structures. Their movements lacked grace and were inhibited. Further, pursuing his theory of libido, he began to focus on "draining" the energy from psychic complexes as the basis of a cure. Without energy, the complex could not express itself and would eventually disintegrate. Following his observations on "bound" energy, Reich theorized that the reason for the restricted movements and tight muscles of his patients was that enormous amounts of energy were being absorbed by these "armored" muscles. Since the body and mind were functionally equivalent in Reich's thought, the function of armored muscles was to absorb energy and restrict energy flow, thus inhibiting the movement necessary for the feeling of pleasure. At some point, due to training and rigid societal restrictions, the patient, and indeed most people, had learned to fear the feeling of pleasure.

But, one may counter, doesn't society need to have rules and rewards and punishments? Isn't it necessary that we have laws so that people won't murder, rape, and pillage? Reich argued that there are consequences for such mass repression. The muscular armoring of an individual while keeping him or her superficially in check, does not extinguish the instinct. Instead, internal pressure builds. As this tension goes unreleased by natural means, such as sex or more personally creative endeavors, unnatural means of expression are sought. Anger grows as the pressure builds and it is finally anger that is expressed. As an example, Reich points to Twentieth Century society with its pornography, violent crime, and dictatorial government.

In contrast, Reich states that more primitive societies living closer to the state of nature are much less riddled with crime and gratuitous violence. He cites the works of anthropologists such as Malinowski[190] to buttress his point.

In this argument Reich again sounds very much like the Taoist masters whom we will discuss shortly. Due to his view of the human being as a bioenergy system, Reich posited that it is the function of the orgasm to release energy imbalances. The true orgasm is a total experience, not simply localized in the genitals. Surrender and self-expression are modeled in this experience, and this coupling of surrender and self-expression is precisely the attitude which, if universal, would be expressed socially in a fulfilling and nurturing society.

As his researches progressed (and I will not elaborate on them here but refer the reader again to my previous book, *The Tao of Bioenergetics* or to Reich's own works, specifically *The Function of the Orgasm*) he began to theorize about a universal energy that expressed itself in sexuality, and which had the ability to cure diseases both mental and physical. Reich called this energy *orgone.*

Based on this theory and a number of experiments which as stated, are more fully developed elsewhere, Reich attempted to concentrate this cosmic *orgone* energy in a number of devices, most notably the "*orgone* accumulator" and the "cloudbuster." The *orgone* accumulator was a simple box of alternating layers of organic and inorganic materials in which a patient would sit. Reich experimented with the use of *orgone* on such diseases as asthma, arthritis, and cancer. The reports of his results are fully and fairly recorded in Reich's own writings which are readily available to the general public.

Due to his cancer research, Reich was arrested and imprisoned by the FDA. He died the night before he was to be released from prison.

A student of Reich's, Alexander Lowen, while eschewing such devices as the *orgone* accumulator and the cloudbuster, continued Reich's work on the body and in the muscles. Lowen's work consisted of exercises that the patients could do to loosen the muscular armoring that Reich spoke about, and to permit a free flow of what Lowen would term "bioenergy." Lowen's *orgone* therapy was called "bioenergetics." Lowen continually asserted that we are our bodies. Our bodies, as with the existential philosophers, are our ways of being in the world. To Lowen, as with Reich, the energetic processes of the body determined what goes on in the mind and vice versa. Also like Reich, Lowen did not see the energy system as necessarily closed and incapable of being increased. However, Lowen was concerned about a rise in the energy level in people who were not ready, since it could lead to anxiety.

Lowen's goal was to reunite the person with his or her body so that he or she might enjoy the life of the body to the fullest possible extent. Again, pleasure was seen as a positive goal. The ability to feel pleasure is indicative of a healthy, total human being. Its by-products are freedom, grace, and beauty. To Lowen, freedom, grace, and beauty are the primary natures of human beings. Again, this emphasis on and trust in nature is quite similar to the point of view of the Taoist sages, and Lowen's use of physical exercise to increase bioenergy flow is close philosophically to Tai Chi.

Also, like the Chinese physicians who we will discuss below, Lowen includes the concept of "spirit" in his psychological calculations. Spirit for Lowen, however, is not something that exists in a dissociated state from the body, but very much as with Aristotle and Aquinas, is the vital and moving principle of the body.

For Lowen, the spirit and the body are united in grace. Gracefulness of bodily movement and expressions are the signs of a healthy nature.

Strangely, but interestingly, Lowen follows Freud's antithesis of power and pleasure. The pursuit of power with its emphasis on the ego, is opposed to the pursuit of pleasure which involves a surrendering of the ego. In all of the systems which we have examined in this chapter, with the possible exception of Freud's, the ego is seen as just one part, an important part, but a part nonetheless, of a larger and more inclusive system. Energy is to be more evenly dispersed and the center of balance of the person more deeply and equally placed than in just one of its psychic organs, the ego. For Lowen and, especially for Jung, this center is called the "Self."

By pursuing pleasure rather than power, and by centering one's energy in a less egotistical and more balanced psychic position, Lowen, Reich, and to some extent Jung, argue that such a person would be naturally incapable of evil, and would by following his or her own real nature, be capable of self-regulation and thus, external limitations such as laws and petty religious prescriptions would be unnecessary.

This is not to say that religion would be eliminated.

Rather by eliminating the need and concerns of the negative and prescriptive limitations of religion, more room would be made for the positive and creative aspects of the religious life. It would be a world under the rule of grace rather than law.

In the East, Chinese philosophy, science, and medicine preceded and paralleled the work of the depth psychologists and bioenergtic clinicians and researchers. As developed in the *Tao of Bioenergetics*, Chinese culture is based on what I have termed the "energy paradigm."

Qi is the bioenergy of China, although as with orgone, the term "bioenergy" may be too limiting. *Qi*, like *orgone*, is an all-pervasive energy that permeates the entire universe. It can appear in many conceptually distinct forms, but it remains one.

The three basic divisions of *Qi* are heavenly *Qi*, earthly *Qi*, and human *Qi*. As expressed in the hexagrams of the *I Ching*, all three types of *Qi* are comingled to create any one moment of time. In China, however, unlike the West, the idea of discrete, enclosed moments is not accepted. Instead, the emphasis is placed on a world that is in a continual stream of change. This emphasis on change is intertwined with the concept of the continuous flow of energy; the energy paradigm, that is at the base of Chinese culture.

Since China is a radically humanistic culture, human *Qi*, or human energy, is included as a co-equal stream in the flow of energy. The question of whether a tree falling in the forest could create a sound without a human ear to hear it, is a meaningless question to the Chinese. There is nothing without the human being. The human is the "completer" of the universe, the heart of the *I Ching* hexagram, uniting heaven and earth, or rather, heavenly *Qi* and earthly *Qi*, within him or herself.

Chinese medicine starts from the concept of *Qi*. While it deals mainly in what is termed human *Qi*, it does acknowledge the influence of the heavenly and earthly *Qi*. Starting from the concept of energy, Chinese physicians, very much like Wilhelm Reich, view the human being *functionally*. In other words, *what* does a particular area of the energy field *do*, as opposed to the isolation of certain physical structures, is the direction of Chinese anatomical inquiry. The "large intestine," for example, is not seen as a long organic tube sitting around the abdomen, but as a set of actions that center around the elimination of waste. Chinese "organs" such as the heart, lungs, kidneys, liver, et cetera, are not distinct physical structures, but groups of functions in the energy field that is the human being.

Chinese medical anatomy, starting as it does with the view of the human being as a field of energy and his or her "organs" as a group of functions, concerns itself with physical structures only secondarily, if at all. The anatomy that Chinese physicians learn and manipulate is the anatomy of the human energy field. Channels, called meridians, run through the energy field connecting organs and providing pathways for the flow of *Qi*. There are twelve major meridians in the human energy field. Along these meridians are hundreds of cavities, or energy switching areas. There are one hundred and eight major cavities. These cavities are accessed by acupuncture needles or by massage and acupressure in order to change, decrease, or increase the flow of *Qi* to certain organs or areas of the energy field. A more thorough explanation of Chinese medicine is provided in the *Tao of Bioenergetics* and in the books of Dr. Yang Jwing-Ming, and will not be explored here, since we are only concerned with the parallel energy concepts of bioenergetics and Chinese medicine and science.

Along with the organs, meridians, and cavities of Chinese medicine, the "eight extraordinary vessels" are also considered. These "vessels" are assigned to certain areas of the human anatomy and store *Qi*. In thinking of Chinese *Qi* anatomy, the meridians have been likened to rivers and the vessels to reservoirs. The reservoirs draw off and store or release energy into the human system as needed.

Qi comes from several sources, but in the human being is produced basically in two places: the bone marrow and the sexual organs. Accordingly, a practice called *Qi Gong* has arisen in China from ancient times which deals in the increased production and conscious direction of *Qi* to achieve goals ranging from better health and longevity to spiritual enlightenment and release. *Qi Gong* is also practiced by Chinese martial artists in both an offensive and defensive manner.

It is a commonplace that the human brain is used only to about one-tenth of its capacity. The *Qi Gong* masters recognize this and attempt to increase the amount and flow of *Qi* in their systems tenfold. This vastly increased supply of *Qi* is eventually directed to the brain and swamps it, forcing open aspects of the mind which are not utilized in everyday consciousness. The mind is broken open and the *Qi* is directed and formed in such a manner as to create a new person, a whole new "spiritual fetus," to which the practitioner's energy will eventually be transferred.

In order to generate this strong a flow of *Qi*, it is obvious that the *Qi* producing centers must be stimulated.

One of the most frequently used paths to increase *Qi* is what is termed "muscle-tendon changing," and "marrow/brain washing" *Qi Gong*. Dr. Yang's book on this subject is highly recommended since it thoroughly explicates the philosophy and exercises utilized in this practice.

Strange as it may seem to Westerners, the primary method of increasing *Qi* is by increasing what is termed "essence" or semen. Semen, according to Chinese *Qi Gong* theory is converted by certain *Qi Gong* meditations and procedures into essence, and then utilized in *Qi* circulation. Essence or *Jing* is, therefore, to be saved and stored for use in *Qi Gong* practice. Accordingly, there is a whole literature of Taoist sexual practices that aim at preserving *Jing* or essence. Both men and women can practice these techniques which aim at using the sex act to increase the production of essence, but then prevent it from "leaking out" from the individual's energy system. Instead, by careful training and discipline, the flow of essence is reversed and is led into the spinal cord to be directed into the esoteric channels of the body and eventually to the brain to "wash" it.

According to Chinese medicine and *Qi Gong* theory, since the human being is an energy system, there is no real division between mind and body. Therefore, all physical ailments and affects have their mental or emotional component and all mental affects have a physical expression. To manipulate one is to manipulate the other. This, of course, sounds very similar to Reich's theories. Like Reich, and for that matter, Lowen, the state of the energy flow of the human being is responsible for the health of the person.

Interestingly, in China, the quality of the energy flow determines not only the mental condition of the person, as one would expect under the bioenergetic theories of Reich or Lowen, but possibly also the moral qualities of the individual. One could be lazy, violent, or aggressive, depending upon the flow, quality, level, balance of yin and yang and, the expression of the five elements in one's energy field. By controlling, directing, and purifying one's energy system then, one's moral expression would naturally become harmonious and benign. This follows the Taoist's philosophy that observes that following nature (in this case the natural flow of *Qi* or energy) rather than law, whether human or divine, one would become a good person and ultimately a sage.

The Taoists, very much like Reich, asserted that people must learn to observe and trust nature — including their own individual nature. Each of us has *Te*, or power; virtue. In order to live the good life, in order to be good — as we naturally are — we must not artificially restrict our *Te*, but give it as much room for self-expression as possible. This is the theory of the "Wind and Stream," or "Romantic" Taoists.[191] Again, the works of Wilhelm Reich parallel those of the Taoists. In his book, *The Invasion of Compulsory Sex Morality*, Reich uses the anthropological studies of Malinowski to demonstrate that in the state of nature, human beings shared all things with one another. Desires were kept to the necessary and responsibilities, which were not needlessly multiplied, were held in common by the community. It was only after the rise of the physical dominance of males and the invention of property that things began to change. People, especially woman and children, became property. From there, the most primitive laws, those dealing with property and domestic relations, developed.

In *The Mass Psychology of Fascism*, Reich dissected the

psychology of the mass man, the follower of the Fascist dictator of his day and found that the unreasonable and overly strict authoritarian family structure produced sexually and creatively blocked individuals whose energies were systematically stopped from free and positive self-expression. Since these energies were artificially inhibited, they could only leak out and express themselves in unnatural ways — through mass sadism and mass destruction.

Energy, therefore, must flow naturally and purely. This is an insight common to both the ancient Taoist sages and the modern energy-oriented depth psychologists.

It should be easy to see at this point that the Latin term *virtue* and the Chinese *Te* are equivalent. Further, the association of virtue, as our analysis showed, with biology, potency, sexuality, and energy, is borne out both by depth psychology, and, by the Chinese explorations and applications of the same term. Shocking as it may sound, therefore, virtue is a concept expressive of sexual potency and natural biological energy.

Now, this insight seems so counter to the moral training that we have received as to appear absurd. However, an open-minded analysis would make many of our religious beliefs more reasonable than they are now.

We can start with Jesus' injunctions to love one another and to love one's neighbor as oneself, and hardest of all, to love our enemies. We all at least intellectually acknowledge that following these injunctions would lead to a better, more peaceful, and fulfilling world. However, even the most ardent Christian finds this, and especially the part about one's enemies, hard, if not impossible to put into practice.

I was a pastor for five years at a small church in rural Ohio. There were many beautiful and spiritual people there. Twice every week we had Bible study. I wish I had a dollar for every time one of the cherubic grandmothers who attended these sessions said that they knew what Jesus had said, but found it hard to forgive their enemies. As for the men, forget it. Grudges were held for generations. This was farm country. Disputes about land were especially serious. I actually had one very dedicated family stop coming to church rather than attend when another family with whom they had a boundary dispute came to the same church.

But Jesus told Peter to forgive his brother seventy times seven times. Paul himself advises that one should "suffer oneself to be defrauded." Why do basically good intentioned people have so much trouble putting such a clear set of principles into action?

Because there is no root. In our discussion of the nature of human beings in the first chapter, we observed that laws or rules that come to human beings from outside are just like any other "thing." They relate to the past. They place erroneous assumptions on the future. They are non-living, and, therefore, inhuman. All that is human comes from the existential structures of the human being. There are no laws, but there is nature — which if one believes in a personal God, is also created by God and thus is good, as stated in *Genesis* — and energy, virtue. This energy or virtue, again because it is natural, is good. It does not move according to externally imposed "laws," but by its own inner dynamics which are life-affirming, life-protective, and inherently creative and self-expressive.

One cannot love if one does not feel love. Simply to tell someone to "love one another" cannot make them do it. I am quite sure Jesus understood this. However, since his mission was to preach the Kingdom of God, in human language, he did his best with the tools at hand. He also taught by example, and the example is just as articulate, if not more so, than his words. This man had no enemies. He forgave everyone. He also promised that everyone could do even greater things than he.

In order to accomplish this, Jesus stated that he would send a helper, a comforter — the Holy Spirit to his followers. This Spirit did come on Pentecost and descended upon the disciples like "tongues of fire." From that date onward his followers, who had been cowering in Jerusalem and hiding since the crucifixion, spread out into the world like an unstoppable wave. This gift of the Spirit is promised to all believers. Even now.

What is the story of Pentecost, however, if not a recogni-

tion that words alone, external "things," are not enough? It is
a recognition that there must be something in the person
him or herself in order for the Kingdom of God to appear on
earth. It has been theorized that when Jesus said that the
Kingdom of God is at hand, he meant from the time of his
birth and with the descent of the Spirit on Pentecost. Spirit
is essential.

This is not a book of theology, but it is to be remembered
that the Chinese in their medicine and their philosophical
practices, include *Shen,* or spirit as an integral part of the
human being. This is also the position of depth psychologists such as Alexander Lowen. It is further the mainstream
Western philosophical position of Aristotle and his follower,
Aquinas. It comports with our conclusion concerning the
composition of the human being and the inclusion of the
mystical and unlimited "person" or *atman/Brahman*, which
is nonetheless partially, in the world. The story of Pentecost
comports very well with these concepts. We all have some
sort of spirit within us. It may or may not be developed.
Energy blockages or misdirected *Qi* flows may inhibit or con-
strict it. However, when one hears beautiful and moving
teachings such as the gospels, the *Qur'an*, the *Bhagavad
Gita*, or the *Sutras of the Buddha*, and one is ready, blockages,
at least temporarily, are loosened. We feel. In that moment,
from whatever source, nature or, if you so believe, God, a
new type of spirit is released. The mind and body, the whole
being is affected. I personally have been in Pentecostal
churches. I personally have had the experience of speaking
in tongues. It is an overwhelmingly joyful experience.

But what happens afterwards? Jesus gave us the parable
of the seeds. Some are scattered on the path and never take
root. Others fall on rocky soil and have shallow roots and
wither in the first heat. And finally, others fall on good soil
and take deep, strong root. As argued by the Chinese sages
and the depth psychologists, there are differences among
people. There must be roots. One's mind/body must be
ready.

What has been our experience of Christianity? How many
bloody, vicious wars have been fought against not only

non-Christians, but among Christians? Whole continents have been conquered by sword, machine gun, and poisonous gas in the name of Christ whose only commandment was that of love. Slavery was justified. The depletion and befouling of the environment was seen as a birthright.

How many times have we turned on the news to hear about yet another Christian minister or priest who has been accused of unnatural sex offenses? Jesus said wisely that many will come mouthing the words "Lord, Lord," but he will sadly have to reply, "I do not know you."

As the following discussion of the Chinese teachings on morality will show, it is only by the enlightened cultivation of our human nature — which, as stated, could very well be our "God-given" nature — that we have any hope at all of becoming the new moral creatures spoken of in the New Testament.

Someone like a Jimmy Swaggert is a prime example of what we are driving at. Mr. Swaggert was uncompromising in condemning evil on his television show. He had no mercy on his colleagues who fell short of his high standards. However, Mr. Swaggert himself was later caught with prostitutes. The sexual acts involved were not simply the acceptable mainstream types of acts practiced by good, middle-class married couples. Instead they involved others performing for Swaggert. Jim Bakker is yet another example. His failings involved not only financial swindles, but illicit sexual conduct involving both males and females.

Strangely enough, I don't doubt the sincerity of these men's dedication to Christianity. However, one is certainly entitled to ask how this Christianity expressed itself in them. Following the theories of Reich and Lowen, it seems quite evident that while both men could assent to the "Good News" of Christianity, the obvious goodness of the path that Christ preached, that is where it stopped. The blockages of energy, the muscular armoring and rigidity of both men, and possibly their sincere belief that they should be all "blocked-up" as a defense against evil, prevented them from expressing their human, God-created nature as intended, that is in a direct, honest, and natural way. Consequently, the energy "leaked," and, following Reich and Lowen, expressed itself in uncritical and unnatural ways. Their actions were compulsive, uncontrollable, and irrational, destroying their entire lives. The "schizoid," or divided personality, to use Lowen's term, that developed from mistaken beliefs caused them to leave their Christian beliefs unconnected and unintegrated with the rest of their being. There must be a root.

In China too, love, in the form of *Jen* or human-heartedness, was the ground of all of the virtues. However, while *Jen* was a philosophical term used by Confucius, it did not stand somewhere above Chinese society, but was incorporated in a much more practical, and ultimately, physical sense. In the discussion that follows, it must be borne in mind that "physical" as used in China includes the mind, body, and spirit. The human being is a continuum, an energy grid or field without the rigid divisions promulgated in the West.

In our discussion of Chinese medicine, we spoke about *Qi* or energy which was the basis of all Chinese science and medicine. The concept of *Qi* is basic to Chinese society and is found not only in medicine and science, but pervades all of Chinese thought and culture. Chinese philosophy and moral philosophy also integrate this concept.

It is readily apparent that the Taoists, with their concerns with nature, longevity, and immortality would be concerned with the workings of *Qi*. The first Taoist sage, Yang Chu, was famous for his quip that he would not pull one hair from his body to save the whole world.[192] This seemingly anti-social and irresponsible comment, however, actually meant that one's first duty is the preservation of the self.[193] Starting points for the Taoists were the preservation of life and the avoidance of injury. Accordingly, the Taoists placed great value on the physical body and its health. Lao Tzu, the author of the *Tao Te Ching*, developed this position further by counseling people that to preserve oneself one must know the laws of change in the universe and adapt to their nature.[194] The Taoists observed that "Reversal is the way of the Tao,"[195] meaning that things tend to progress to an extreme, but once that extreme is reached, the energy of the universe begins again to balance itself by progressing towards its opposite. This process continues into infinity.[196]

Therefore, one should adopt the "middle way" in one's life, avoiding extremes and being neither good nor bad.[197] This is a naturalistic morality. The injunction of Lao Tzu to know nature was the starting point of Chinese science and medicine. The systematic study of the laws of nature was begun. *Qi*, being the basic paradigm of the Chinese,[198] predates even the Taoists and is the basis of the oldest Chinese classic, the *I Ching*.[199] The Taoist scientists and physicians extensively studied *Qi*, and incorporated their findings on its laws and movements into their philosophical framework.

Knowing that the universe is subject to continual change, the final step in Taoism was taken by Chuang Tzu, who advocated that one view things from the point of view of the Tao. The Tao itself was not a "thing" and was therefore unchanging.

Not quite as obvious as the Taoist interest in *Qi* and the medical model of morality, was the Confucian interest in the same matter. Where the Taoists emphasized nature, the Confucians began with relationships; specifically human relationships. The reason for this need to form relationships, Confucius asserted, was *Jen* or love.[200] *Jen* is also translated as "human-heartedness" or "compassion." However, I use the term "love" due both to its reverberations with the teachings of Christ, in which its use is very similar, and since, like "love," it runs the gamut in its connotations from sexuality, to romance, to *agape,* or platonic love. It, therefore, has more of a resonance with the Western mind and loses nothing in accuracy.

According to the Confucians, *Jen* represents the human heart, and its counterpart, *yi*, or righteousness, represents the human way or path. It is to be remembered that for the Chinese, the "heart" is not merely the material muscle found in the chest, but is defined functionally to include the emotions and the mind. Thoughts and emotions are not separated for the Chinese. This, of course, prevents the schizoid problem that one encounters so frequently in the West where the mind, or at least the so-called "rational" part of it is artificially and arbitrarily "separated" from the body and the emotions.

Yi is also defined as "oughtness." It is one's duty.[201] *Jen* is the reason for duty. Because we love, we must meet our responsibilities to others. This is not a burden placed upon us from outside, but is a gift we willingly give to those we love. Remember back to one of your biggest "crushes." Would you have denied that person anything? Didn't you spend your time thinking of things you could do for him or her, or gifts you would like to give them? This is the spirit of Confucian "duty" or *Yi*. A person who expresses these virtues is termed a "*Man of Jen.*"[202]

Like the Taoists who attempted to view things in a detached, natural mode, that is, from the point of view of the Tao, the Confucians also attempted to view things more universally, meaning not some sort of platonic abstraction, but rather from the cultivated experience of combining the energies of heaven and earth in man just as in the hexagrams of the *I Ching*.[203] Such a person was called *T'ien Min* or a "citizen of Heaven."[204]

There are four basic Confucian virtues: *Jen* or love, *Yi* or righteousness, propriety and wisdom.[205] The Man of *Jen* tries to express these virtues in his life. Although there are four virtues, however, *Jen* is their basis and encompasses all of them.[206] That is why the virtuous man is called a "Man of *Jen*," or, a "man of love" in Western terms.

Jen is expressed in two ways: *Chung* and *shu. Chung,* or "seriousness, conscientiousness" is the positive expression of *Jen* and moves one to do for others what you would wish them to do for you. *Shu* or altruism is the negative respect of *Jen* and directs one not to do to others what you wouldn't have them do to you.[207] As with the Taoists, practical morality enjoined one to follow the Doctrine of the Mean or *Chung Yung,* and avoid extremes in one's behavior and attitude.[208] Again, this flows easily from the detached and universal view of the *T'ien Min.*

It would seem that Confucianism with its basis in love is very much like Christianity without the theology. However, such a view would be mistaken. In Christianity, all goodness, all virtue comes upon humankind from the *outside*; from God. In Confucianism, as with Taoism, goodness comes from *inside.* Goodness is the human being's original nature.

Confucius' most well known follower, Mencius, declared that it was human nature to be good. Mencius argues that all men and women possess the "four beginnings," that is, the beginnings of the four virtues in their nascent state as "feelings." These feelings are shame and dislike, modesty and yielding, and right and wrong.[209] From the "feelings" are developed the four virtues. Although a human being is good he or she can, however, be trained or learn to be evil. Thus evil, not goodness, comes from the outside. This is why the Confucians were so concerned with politics, government, and public service. Society exists because of the natural human drive to form loving relationships. Government and culture must express that nature. The purpose of public service, therefore, is love and the prevention of evil influences that would pervert essentially good nature. This is also why learning and education were the cornerstones of the Confucian or *Ju* (scholarly) school.

We can see then that although there are differences in emphasis in the two major philosophical families or "Chia" of China, growing from the same soil, there are remarkable similarities. For our purposes the recognition that the virtuous person follows nature is extremely important. In nature is to be found virtue. Mencius stated that to know one's heart (mind) was to know one's nature. To know one's nature was to know heaven.[210] This is the same insight as our classical linguistic investigations and our explorations of depth psychology. In Confucianism, as well as Taoism, therefore, the pursuit of virtue leads to *Qi*.

In the long history of China there were originally the "Hundred Schools" of philosophy. One of these was the Legalist School. The Legalists took a position that was the diametric opposite of that which we have been expounding in our study of Taoism and Confucianism. The Legalists rejected virtue and argued that it was only law that made one good. Good was defined by the Legalists as fitting into society and following the dictates of the law. In many respects this was a behavioral state since the Legalists were only interested in public behavior. The Legalists accordingly

were called *Fang Shu Chih Shih*, or "Men of Method."
Legalism was the "method" of handling people. As long as
the "method" was applied consistently, society would function well.

The Legalists, following the philosopher Han Fei Tzu and
Li Ssu, the prime minister, gained control of a united China
under the Ch'in Dynasty. Although this dynasty was
short-lived, it did manage to destroy the vast majority of the
"Hundred Schools." Only the Confucianists and Taoists were
strong enough to survive into the following dynasties. Being
the only surviving schools, and faced with a challenge from a
foreign source, Buddhism, the two schools adopted ideas
and concepts from each other. Therefore, the original
schools of Confucianism and Taoism became the hybrids of
Neo-Confucianism and Neo-Taoism.[211]

Neo-Taoism took a "romantic" turn in the *Feng Liu* movement. The *Feng Liu*, literally, "wind and stream," emphasized
living with "elegance" and freedom. This was done by living
according to *Tzu Jan* or the spontaneous, in the sense of
doing what comes "naturally" to one. In this sense *Feng Liu*
was unlike other forms of Taoism since it was irrational and
impulsive. Wang Pi, the philosopher of this movement of
Taoism, asserted that the sage has emotions, in fact,
stronger, more deeply felt emotions that respond to more
subtle stimuli than those of the average person. However,
being a sage, he or she while appreciating his emotions and
feelings, is not overcome by them.[212] In the West we would
recognize the ideas of the *Feng Liu* as similar to those of the
Romantic movement of Byron, Shelly, and Keats. From this
Romantic emphasis on natural, spontaneous feelings came
the Chinese version of courtly love, which in the West was to
flower in medieval Europe and to be later idealized in the
writings of European romantics such as Walter Scott.

The Neo-Confucians also came closer to the naturalistic
tenets of the Taoists. While maintaining their emphasis on
relationships and culture, the argument that it is human
nature to be virtuous led the Neo-Confucians, like their
Taoist brethren, to an exploration of *Qi*.

The Neo-Confucians held, as did their forbearers, that

▶ ▶

the sage was a *dynamic* person acting with virtue in society.[213] Therefore, following Taoist science and medicine, they tended to emphasize the physical element in the universe.[214] That element was *Qi*.[215]

Shao Yung developed a cosmological theory based on the cycles of the hexagrams of the *I Ching*, and the waxing and waning of yin and yang. Cheng Tsai (1020-1077) followed and based his cosmology on the cycles of *Qi*. The *I Ching* thus was a natural energy cycle.[216]

Of course the human being, as united with heaven and earth, and permeated with *Qi*, was also subject to these cycles. The Neo-Confucians thus developed their own cosmology in which they split the universe into *Qi* and *Li*. *Qi*, of course, is natural energy; *Li*, the form that this energy takes. All things are a combination of *Qi* and *Li*, very much as the world of Aristotle was a combination of form and substance.[217]

It follows, therefore, that to be embodied, a human being needs *Qi*. It is a person's *Qi* that makes him or her an individual human being instead of some abstract idea. *Qi* is the person's physical endowment; *Li*, his or her nature, or essence. Like the Neo-Taoists, the Neo-Confucians believed that the quality of a person's *Qi* made one what one was. Clear, strong *Qi* was that of a potential sage. Turbid *Qi*, that of a fool. Under this scheme, following Mencius, *Li*, or nature, is good, but one's *Qi* can make one evil.[218]

It is important to note that *Li* is not the same thing as mind. *Li* is human nature. It is abstract and not active, but contains the four beginnings described by Mencius. Mind occurs only with the combination of *Qi* and *Li*, energy and nature. Mind is active and must be used to develop the four beginnings into the four virtues.[219]

Because the man of *Jen* knows that all things are part of the cycle of *Qi*, which cannot be changed, these things belong to the realm of *Ming* or Fate. Therefore, the sage goes about his or her normal duties with conscientiousness, and expresses *Jen* by doing his or her very best for others. This is the only thing over which he or she has control.[220]

With the inclusion and study of *Qi* in both schools, we

can see how *Qi Gong* practice would appeal to the practitioners of both. Also, by making virtue dependent upon nature and energy, the schools have physicalized virtue as our original discussion postulated. For such a thing as virtue to be possible or to have any meaning, it must come from within the human being him or herself, and it must have roots, as our study of bioenergy has shown, in the physical body. However, the term physical body is meant something like the energy matrix, including body, mind, and spirit, as used in Chinese medicine and *Qi Gong* practice. If virtue does not come from within, we are left with the Legalist definition, which has no place for ethics of any sort.

We find, based upon the derivations and formations of the term "virtue" and its related words, our investigation of Western depth psychology, especially the works of Wilhelm Reich and Alexander Lowen, and, finally, our study of Chinese medical and *Qi Gong* philosophy, that virtue means power, strength, and energy, and specifically, sexual energy.

At this point we know that the human being is a composite of a body which is a quasi-object in the world, and a transcendent, but embodied, component that is beyond subjectivity and objectivity called the "person," *atman/Brahman*. This "person" is not a thing and has the power to negate things as they are. It is totally free but its embodiment is involved with and an expression of bio-sexual cosmic energy. Because the human being is embodied, it must exist in the world. As such, it is subject to things beyond its control. These things are called *Ming* or Fate. The human being must meet fate or *Ming*, and the only way he or she can do this is by exercising inner strength, or virtue. Virtue is the power of the bio-sexual energy of the universe and the earth as combined in the energy matrix that is the human being. Virtue, bio-sexual energy, allows man to love. Love is the basis of all the virtues. Virtue gives one the ability, the power, the will and the strength to act ethically.

We have also seen in our study of human being that it is human nature to be creative. As Mencius the Chinese sage also argued, it is human nature to be virtuous and to act ethically. Ethics then is a species of creativity, and, as we have seen, is also related to art. The only distinction is that while art, like the law, need not be beautiful, ethical actions, based as they are on virtue, and thus bio-sexual energy, must always express grace and freedom. They must be beautiful.

In the first chapter we argued that ethics, like art, must be conscious. Following principles of depth psychology we asserted that in order to act consciously, there must be sufficient energy, or virtue, to bring an ethical question above the line of consciousness. This energy is only produced by tension. This is the tension of opposites spoken of by Jung. Nothing produces tension like conflict. Therefore, while *Ming* or fate provides the possibility of opposition, and virtue, the necessary energy to meet it, both *Ming* and virtue are only components of ethics. That is, while they make ethics possible, it is only in actual conflict that ethical decisions and behaviors occur.

It is a commonplace, of course, that strength can be increased by exercise. Accordingly we have everything from weight-lifting to *Qi Gong*. It is in the life of the warrior where the training for the increasing of strength and the eventual facing of conflict are combined. It is in the way and art of the warrior that virtue is put to use in conflict. This way is called *Bushido*, and from it is derived the spiritual arts and ways of *Budo*.

CHAPTER FOUR

Budo: The Art of the Applied Use of Energy

I have a colleague named Larry. Now, "Larry" is not his real name but a nom de guerre that I'm using for this chapter on conflict. Granted, it's not a really good nom de guerre, like "Lancelot," or "Sulieman the Magnificent," or even "Vlad the Impaler," but "Larry" will do. After all, Larry is a defense attorney.

I first met Larry while doing trial work for the Prosecutor's Office. Life was simple then. I would meet with the defense attorney before trial and try to negotiate a reasonable plea agreement. If we couldn't agree, we went to trial.

Larry, however, did not operate that way. He burst into my office unannounced, informed me that I hadn't complied with the Local Rules of Court, the Rules of Criminal Procedure, the spiritual exercises of Ignatius Loyola, and the Code of Hammurabi. Then he demanded my entrails.

Of course, my entrails are dear to me so he wasn't getting them. But all in all, it was a masterful performance. I, however, also use strategy. In dealing with aggressive defense attorneys like Larry, I play stupid and stall. Why I've been known to drag my feet up beyond jury selection in a trial. I agree with everything defense counsel says. Admit that I am a stupid and worthless person. Throw filth on myself on the cathedral steps — and secretly prepare for trial. One rule of trial attorneys — there is nothing but the trial.

▶ ▶

So Larry did his maneuvering and I did mine. This particular trial involved four dopers in a car. Larry's client was one of them. The dope was on the floor. The question was "Whose dope was it?" For some reason, the grand jury indicted Larry's client. Ah, where would we be without the stout yeomen we place on our juries!

Needless to say, there was absolutely no evidence pointing to Larry's client as opposed to any of the other occupants of the car. Larry's client walked.

Strangely enough, actually not that strangely since this often happens once a trial actually starts, Larry and I had some pleasant conversations in the trenches and developed a mutual respect. There are two types of lawyers: Those who are willing to go to trial and those who are not. If it gets out that you are afraid to go to trial, you will be a victim your entire career. However, once you've gone to trial with a person, you get at least a modicum of respect from him or her. And you deserve it.

The next time I saw Larry's doper client, he had killed a man. It was a drug shoot-out at a housing project. Larry's client and his assistant marketing representative were having a turf dispute with two other entrepreneurs. Guns were drawn and a gunfight ensued where people lived and children played. One man was playing cards. He decided to go to the store for pizza and beer. He opened his screen door. It was his last act in this world.

The victim was hit in the chest with a nine millimeter slug. It yanked out his heart, ripped out his lungs, tore his spleen, and lodged in his right shoulder. Guns are something everyone should have around the house, aren't they?

When the police investigated, they found that luckily, each participant in the gunfight had a different caliber gun. Find the man with the nine millimeter and you find the killer. Of course, it turned out that everyone involved in the fight gave evidence indicating that Larry's client, the doper, was the man with the "nine." The police obtained a videotaped statement from the doper's partner who had been shot in the fight. The partner put the "nine" in the doper's hot little hand.

Speaking of partners, some background of my meteoric career is needed at this point. In Montgomery County, Ohio, two county prosecutors are assigned to each of our eleven trial judges. We divide the case load so no one is swamped with trials. My partner, to whom this case was originally assigned, quit to become a federal judge. Before leaving, she assigned the case to another attorney named Irving (also a nom de guerre).

Irving was a man of many interests. Few of them related to his job as a prosecutor. It was, accordingly, rare to see Irving in the office. However, I did manage to see him on a couple of occasions after my former partner had assigned this trial to him. Irving graciously informed me on both occasions that "We have a tough trial coming up soon. We have to talk. See you later. We'll talk." Who was that masked man?

It wasn't my case. I was scheduled for eight trials in seven weeks. So I didn't think much of it. Irving was a senior attorney, and if he needed me to run a few errands or second-seat the trial, fine. I did not realize how close this major trial was.

On one of his flying visits to the office, Irving informed me (as he was leaving) that the trial would start in ten days. Ten days! When would he be back? Had subpoenas been sent? No subpoenas. Didn't know when we'd talk. By the way, he'd be in South Carolina the weekend before the trial. Start the trial without him. He'd be there by Tuesday or Wednesday.

I am not a brave man, as I've repeatedly stated in this book. However, the fear of looking like a fool at trial is a greater fear to me than any other. I dropped everything else and interviewed cops, witnesses, doctors, and the coroner. I viewed evidence — including those breath-taking slides at the Coroner's Office — and, of course, Larry kept up his demands and motions the entire time. Once he had found that I was the target, he zeroed in. Dance cowboy. Bang, bang.

The opening day of what would be a five-day trial arrived. I picked a jury. I made the opening statement. Larry made his. He attacked my case. He attacked the cops. He had a chart clearly proving that all of those stories about my ancestry were true. We began the evidence.

About this time Irving showed up. "Get 'em tiger!" was his advice.

Larry's defense was self-defense. His client, the doper, hadn't intended to plug the innocent victim. No, he was merely defending himself. He had only intended to plug his rival. And Larry had an ace up his sleeve. The Friday before trial, he appeared unannounced in my office to inform me that the doper's partner, of video confession fame, had recanted, and further, to prove his case of self-defense, said partner had been shot and the bullet had miraculously worked its way out of his leg, this very week, right before trial. Thank you Jesus! Larry dropped the bullet on my desk and demanded that we have it tested in the Crime Lab at county expense.

At this point, Larry and I, who are both into heraldry, discussed *his* ancestry. Then I threw him out.

But back to the trial itself.

As the State's evidence proceeded, it was becoming clear that Larry's claim of self-defense was not going to fly. He did every guerrilla tactic that a defense attorney could do. He objected to every witness. He accused Irving and me of withholding evidence from him. I called him a liar on the official record. He did the same for me. We yelled at each other and threatened each other in court and in the judge's chambers. This was all great fun. Irving, however, was genuinely angry. He and Larry got into a grudge match on the third day of the trial. Since Irving was the senior counsel on the case, he took over the trial. I got to sit out the remainder of the case.

Irving, lest one get the wrong impression of him, was for all his faults, a superb trial attorney. His problem was that he loved to taunt his opponents by blatantly refusing to prepare for trial — and then win nonetheless. It only hurts his opponents worse to see that while they kill themselves in preparing, Irving, who has spent the weekend before trial with his girlfriend in Florida, has waltzed in and clobbered them. And Irving has never been a good winner. He sneers condescendingly at his vanquished foes. He carries a gun.

At any rate, the grudge match began. Nobody could talk sense to either attorney. They sniped, they fought, they insulted each other for three whole days.

On Thursday, we caved in and had Larry's bullet analyzed. The doper's friend testified he and the doper had been fired upon; that he had been shot; that they were afraid and only fired back in self-defense. The bullet in his leg had worked its way out and he, a State's witness, and only motivated by a thirst for justice, had gone to the doper's defense attorney — Larry — and told him all of this, providing him with said bullet.

Irving and I came back from lunch early to find the lab technician in the hall. He had a puzzled look on his face.

"Did you guys say that someone was shot with this bullet?"

"Yeah."

"This bullet has never been in a human body. There's no discoloration on it like there should be."

Irving and I choked, and laughed, and rolled on the floor — but we didn't tell Larry. It was his test, after all. Let him find out the good news himself.

When we were again in the courtroom, Irving called the lab man. Larry did not object and appeared expansive and was certainly gloating. He had us — he thought. Then the lab guy dropped his bomb. Larry, momentarily flinched. Irving smirked. Larry regained himself and objected. The judge laughed.

Larry now changed tactics. Self-defense, bah. It was really the doper's friend, he, who had so recently helped Larry, who had evilly misled us all! It was the friend, not the doper, who had actually had the "nine," and had killed the victim. Larry was too good to ever drop the ball.

On the morning of the last day of trial, I was in the courtroom early. Larry took me aside. He told me that he had evidence to totally destroy our case. As a courtesy to me, he said that I should step back and let Irving take the blast. I told him that I appreciated his telling me this, but his man was guilty and we had to get him. He said he respected me for that. We shook hands and the war began again as soon as

Irving entered.

What Larry had was two female friends of the doper and his partner who testified that they had seen the partner with a nine millimeter earlier the day of the shooting. He also had an independent witness who said she saw a man running from the shooting with a big gun in his hand. The man she described was dressed like the partner. Not the doper. I thought we were dead.

During closing arguments, however, I was flipping through the transcript and found that the "independent" witness had made a critical mistake. Everyone had testified that the doper's friend had been shot in the right leg. The doper had been shot in the left foot. The man the witness described was dragging his left leg! I shoved this into Irvin's hands. An evil grin crossed his face. It blew their whole case.

We won. But it could have gone the other way. In another phase of the moon, or with a higher tide, the jury would have believed the defense witnesses. But on this day we won. It was a bitter, bloody, dirty, nasty, hard-fought, no quarter battle.

Two days later Larry and I had lunch. He helped me with a private project I was doing, and I wished him luck in the polo match he was going to play in India. There is a code of conduct in battle. Nobody, not me, not Larry, not Irving, had crossed that line in this bitter fight. We are all professionals.

Now Larry is a good trial attorney. He's intelligent, articulate, evil, and blood-thirsty. Larry does not have to be coddled. A fight with him is all-out. But there are other lawyers who are not that competent. They are treated differently. That is also part of the code.

There is a judge in our courthouse who never grants continuances. It doesn't matter whether a key witness is missing or evidence is being developed — the trial goes on when he sets it. No exceptions. Consequently, the attorneys who serve on his docket get swamped and occasionally have to cover trials for one another.

One Monday afternoon my partner and I were casually speaking to the judge when he turned to my partner and said that he had two trials set for Tuesday, the next day. Who would be covering the breaking and entering trial since my partner couldn't be in two places at one? My partner asked for a continuance. Nonsense, why, George can do it. I felt a warm trickle down by pant leg.

The next morning I was in trial on a case I had only received the afternoon before. Thank God the witnesses had all been subpoenaed. Never mind that I had never met them, let alone prepped them for trial.

The defendant had a twenty-year history of petty crimes. Thefts, break-ins. Nothing violent, nothing dangerous. He was mainly an annoyance, and was borderline retarded with severe behavioral problems. His attorney also fit that description.

How this woman passed the bar exam was one of the mysteries of the universe. How she found her way to the courtroom was more puzzling still. She was a nice person, but not terribly competent. She was, in short, no Larry.

In the State of Ohio, a prosecutor can comment on the past criminal convictions of a defendant; but only the felony convictions; and only the felony convictions that have occurred within the last ten years. I had looked at this guy's record and while he had a couple of felonies, they had occurred back in the 1970s. He had a slew of misdemeanors, but nothing I could use. So, in opening argument, I was forced to stick with the facts of the case. Drat.

The defendant's attorney, however, went into the defendant's record *ad nauseam* for the jury. Thank you, Jesus! She also admitted he was in the pawn shop where the break-in occurred, but that he was only there to keep warm.

Okay, since she did most of my job for me, all I had to prove was that he had attempted to commit a theft in the pawn shop. Unfortunately for me, there was no evidence to support this idea. Undaunted, I put the owner of the shop on the stand, who noted that a drum set had been moved a few inches. Good enough. The bum was obviously trying to steal it, ladies and gentlemen of the jury.

Defense counsel put the defendant on the stand. He could barely speak in English sentences. Remember, I could not ask him about his record. Once again, defense counsel had him confirm each and every misdemeanor and the felonies from the 1970s. Thanks again.

The police claimed to have photos of the hole that the defendant broke in the window to get into the shop. I was elated until I saw it. As a colleague said, you couldn't shove a cat, let alone a human being, through that hole. Nice work, guys. My heart sank. This by itself was enough to create reasonable doubt.

Nonetheless, the guy was convicted. When I went back to thank the jury, they said that they wouldn't have convicted the guy except that his attorney had said that he was such a bad person.

Usually when a prosecutor is forced into a jury trial, we demand that the defendant go to jail. In this case, the judge felt that due to the defendant's obvious mental deficiencies, he needed to be placed in the custody of his family and given mental health treatment. My partner wanted to demand the jail time. I let it go. The guy was not dangerous, just annoying. It wasn't his fault that his court-appointed lawyer was a dud. It is not fair to take undue advantage. It gets you a bad reputation, and it simply does not feel good. Again, there is a code. There are times when it's appropriate to be lenient.

In the first chapter we argued that ethical behavior was the product of conflict, and that conflict had to be conscious in order for the resulting behavior to be called "ethical." Behavior that is simply habitual and automatic cannot be termed ethical. There are two reasons for this, as we discovered in our research into both human being and virtue.

The nature of human being is freedom. The human being, it is true, is a continuum stretching from the physical world of "things" into the realm of "subjectivity" and beyond, into a type of existence transcending both subject and object. While the physical body of the human being is subject to the laws of physics and chemistry, and, while the part that exists as pure subjectivity is largely controlled by "psychological" factors running from overt behavioral control through something like Freud's "mind"; id, ego, and superego, perhaps even into Jung's collective unconscious; the part of the human being that transcends subject and object is existentially free and indefinable. This resulting sense of freedom permeates the other parts of the continuum that is a human being, and makes him or her essentially human, and makes ethical behavior possible. One can choose to act in undetermined ways. One can choose to act against one's own interest. One can choose to act beautifully.

Beauty is a product of the freedom that human beings inject into the world. To be human, one must express his or her freedom. The person, however, lives in a world of physical objects and other subjects or minds. This world is largely beyond the control of the individual human being and is thus ruled by Fate or *Ming*. The human being attempts to participate in this world of *Ming* by uniting his or her freedom with portions of it. This union of freedom and *Ming* is called "art."

Art may be any combination of human freedom and *Ming*. Ethics, by being a product of freedom acting in the world, is a type of art. However, while art itself need not be beautiful, ethical behavior must.

Since ethics is a form of art, and since art requires freedom of action, it is obvious that unconscious habitual behavior can produce neither art nor ethics.

There is, however, a partially unconscious aspect or rather, precondition, to ethics — virtue. Virtue, as we have seen, is a code word for biosexual potency and the bioenergy created from it. This bioenergy gives strength and power to the human being. Since the human being attempts to operate and create in a world that by nature resists his or her efforts, for the human being to express his or her freedom to create, he or she must have the necessary strength and power to make a "place" or "space" of their own in the world. The only way to meet *Ming* is with virtue, as the Confucian scholars proclaimed.

Virtue, however, would be just another blind force of nature were it not for the fact that it can be both increased and consciously directed. As we saw in our discussions of Chinese medicine, a human being is actually a matrix of energy channels. This energy is called *Qi* and its quality, quantity, and level affect the health, both mental and physical, of the individual human being. While doctors skilled in bioenergetic medicine such as the Chinese can externally treat a patient's *Qi* flow, human beings are also capable of consciously affecting and guiding their own *Qi*. This practice is called *Qi Gong* and is used to purify one's *Qi*, increase its level, and direct its flow for spiritual ends.

Although it is arguably possible to have virtue and behave ethically without some sort of meditative or *Qi Gong* practice, such behavior is sporadic at best and basically "rootless." This rootlessness leads to all sorts of hypocrisy and brutality in the name of morality and religion. Morality and religion, of course, are not bad in themselves, but a failure to understand the preconditions for such things leads to unspeakable evils such as witch trials, book burnings, and inquisitions.

"Virtue" is a term strongly derived from biology, as shown. The concept of virtue having roots and flowering is not, therefore, out of line. To push the botanical metaphor further, however, decorative plants must be shaped and formed. This is the basis of the botanical arts from the rose garden to the bonsai forest. Virtue must be guided. The proper guidance of one's virtue comes from constant practice. Practice is not simply rote repetition. It requires concentration and self-observation. Any athlete or martial artist would agree. The conscious direction of energy is accomplished through *Qi Gong* practice. Again, therefore, unconscious, habitual behavior is excluded as a basis for virtue.

While practice, which I will call "*Qi Gong*" since it is an ancient term signifying the control and direction of energy, is necessary to direct energy, one must also be cognizant of the type of energy one is directing. As Chinese physicians, *Qi Gong* masters, and Neo-Confucian scholars have observed, the quality or purity of one's *Qi* determines one's character. It is a part of *Qi Gong* training, therefore, to resolve any problem and to exorcise any emotional imbalances, any disease, to calm one's *Qi*, and, to allow it to flow smoothly.

This, in many respects, is similar to the psychotherapies of Wilhelm Reich and Alexander Lowen. However, while both Reich and Lowen allow for the increase of bioenergy in the human system, except in cases of depression, the increase of bioenergy in and of itself is not necessarily a goal of the therapy.

In *Qi Gong*, however, the increase of *Qi* is an absolute necessity for the achievement of the higher, spiritual levels of the practice. As stated earlier, the increase in *Qi* most successfully comes from the sexual organs and requires stimulation either physically or mentally or both. Stimulation causes tension and tension produces more and more energy to keep the system in balance. The increased energy is then consciously channelled for use in the higher centers of the human energy matrix.

Carl Jung recognized this role of tension in his work on alchemy. Opposite parts of the psyche compete for energy so as to become conscious and to express themselves in the world. An unconscious function absorbing this energy will be felt as a threat. The conscious function will then respond by absorbing energy in the form of a defense mechanism. All human psyches are dynamic energy systems and, accordingly, they are continuously going through this process to a greater or lesser extent. The healthy personality eventually strikes a balance, allowing the unconscious function to express itself and the conscious functions to avoid being overwhelmed.

In dreams and in alchemical literature, Jung found this distribution of energy to be represented as a battle or tension of opposites.[221] The goal of alchemy as with psychotherapy was to synthesize the opposites into a higher union; a new state of being.

This again brings us to conflict. Purifying and increasing one's *Qi*, or virtue, is one thing; existing in the world is quite another. One can be virtuous, but one must still act. Acting or expressing one's freedom in the world necessarily involves resistance from Fate or *Ming* and this conflict is the nature of being-in-the-world.

We all intuitively feel the conflict of existence. In fact, one religion, Buddhism, begins from this very point. One of the four noble truths is that existence is suffering. Suffering can be anything, of course, from living in Bosnia or Somalia, to

▶ ▶

sitting in your penthouse overlooking Central Park and being unhappy with the view. The biggest conflict, and one that also goes to the root of human being, is death. We are temporally limited beings. Everything is done against a backdrop of death. There is always the pervasive conflict with the clock.

So how do we as conflicted beings live? How can we act and express ourselves in and against a resisting world? This is where ethics begins.

Ethics imply action. Action, as pointed out by Sartre, requires choice, and, limitation. But this progressive limitation also entails the creation of an edifice, an essence — one's life. While the laws of bioenergetics leave open the possibility of unconscious conflict, the life produced by such a conflict almost cannot be termed "human." Consciousness is required so that the human being can express his or her most human essence — freedom. The human freedom to create.

We have found that external "laws," "things," are incompatible with human freedom and, therefore, cannot be the basis of ethics, which is a human creation. This has been borne out by our study of virtue, which is an internal energy or power. But if religion and law cannot be the standards of ethical behavior, what can?

As we stated in the first chapter, there is one group of human beings that always and everywhere have an acute understanding of the nearness of death — the warriors; the soldiers. It is true that priests and ministers may try constantly to remind us of death, but we can anesthetize ourselves to their blandishments. However, the one profession in which the nearness of death is constantly felt and, for which the profession itself exists, is that of the warrior. Accordingly, the codes and philosophies of the warrior class are the most appropriate models for ethical behavior.

This is not to say, however, that there existed at any place or time a list of rules for warriors. It has been asserted that the knights of medieval Europe, for example, did not have a code so much as an agenda.[222] What is meant by this will become clearer if we use examples of actual warrior classes.

As we stated earlier, Japan is and was a society in which art was expressed in even the minutest of everyday activities. This striving for perfection, however, is not merely some sort of unconscious, racial trait. It is the product of constant and conscious repetition and training and, a conscious choice to create a society after a certain image of the beautiful. The impetus for this image comes from many sources; Confucius, Mencius, Shinto, but these sources, in Japan, were tied together by a certain class; the Samurai. *Bushido*, the code of the samurai, is the soul of Japan.[223]

Medieval Japan, like medieval Europe was a state enmeshed in political confusion. A state of constant warfare between competing feudal clans was an everyday reality of the Japanese people. Originally, as in Europe, a warrior class emerged. Actually, at this early stage, the term "class" is a misnomer. To be a member of a class requires some sort of class-consciousness. Instead, prior to the Twelfth Century, a group of the more hardy and warlike of the citizenry emerged as warriors. They were called by the Sino-Japanese term *buke* or *bushi*.[224]

The bushi were a rough and rugged breed very similar to the semi-barbaric "knights" of the dark ages in Europe. They are a halfway house between the barbarian warrior and the knight.

As the *bushi* became more and more specialized as warriors proper, and more and more professional in their approach to their calling, the individual warrior felt more of a kinship with his fellow warriors than with the other members of Japanese society; the merchants and farmers. As these men continued to come into contact with each other in war, a code of fair fighting arose.[225] This code is called *bushido*, that is, *bu-shi-do*, or, "fighting knight way."[226] *Bushido* was the precepts of knighthood and gave the bushi guidance in the ways of fighting and the ways to conduct themselves in everyday life.[227]

To see *bushido* as a "code" like the Code Napoleon or some other collection of "laws" is incorrect. *Bushido* is casuistic; that is, it proceeds by precedent. *Bushido* is unwritten and unuttered. It consists of deeds. It is an active code written in the heart growing organically in the experience of the knight rather than being imposed from outside.[228]

Bushido owed its rise and influence to the ascendancy of Yoritomo in the Twelfth Century, during the wars between the Taira and Minimoto clans. It came to fruition during the Tokugawa Era.[229] The influence of *Bushido* also coincides with the rise of a distinct group with a class consciousness — the samurai.

The word "samurai" originally denoted an attendant or a guard.[230] Eventually, as in Europe, the term incorporated overtones of nobility. It was natural, therefore, that a group to which facing death was its reason to exist should see itself as different from and superior to the rest of society. The samurai would stand out because of his arms, but also because of his moral superiority. He was not a man engaged in petty matters. As such, he comported himself as one who was different and superior not only because he could fight, but in everything that he did. His was a life different in every respect from the run of society. Accordingly, he had to internalize the ways of his class so that he would always act like a samurai.

As we stated, *Bushido* was the code of the samurai, and it was an internal, unwritten code. Being unwritten, however, did not mean that it had no foundation; no sources. *Bushido* was grounded not only in technical fighting skills and the camaraderie of any warrior group, but in the spirit of Buddhism and Shinto, and, the moral guidelines of Confucianism.[231]

Buddhism, of course, was developed in India. It spread to China and then to Korea and Japan. In Japan it took many forms, but the one most associated with Japan by Westerners is Zen. We will discuss Zen at more length below, but for the present it is only important to note that Buddhism, with its doctrines of suffering and of the pointlessness of the intellectual examination of life, gave the Japanese people a feeling for submission to the inevitable; a calm trust in fate that fit very well with the spirit of a warring people.

One might ask how this could be when one, starting from

the proposition that there is no self, no "ego," and that the reality we perceive is real but also illusory and, the only peace is through compassion and ultimate release, could just as easily become an ascetic and retire from any participation in the world? The point is that in many ways the life of a professional warrior is also an ascetic life. The soldier must learn to deprive him or herself; to face hardship and, ultimately, death. If all is equally real or illusory, one might just as well act as be passive. Death being as illusory as life, one's death makes no more nor less difference than one's life. One might just as well die as live. An armed person with this attitude is a very formidable opponent.

Shinto is the other religion of Japan. Shinto is a national religion. It revered nature, thus endearing the land and its flora and fauna to the Japanese, much like the Plains Indians centered their worship and culture around the plains and the buffalo and game that roamed on them.[232]

Ancestor worship was the other element of Shinto and through the worship of common ancestors, Shinto brought everyone into one family and linked them all, no matter how humble, to the Imperial Family.[233] This reverence for the land and for the ancestors who lived upon that land gave the Japanese people a strong sense of patriotism and loyalty.[234] The Japanese lived in the land of the gods, and were all personally related to the gods. Therefore, the defense of Japan was akin to the defense of a vast religious shrine. This attitude is again, very much like the Native Americans' attitude toward the Black Hills, which were also held sacred as the place of the gods and the ancestors.

Combining intense and almost religious patriotism and loyalty with a calmness in the face of death made the Japanese possibly the most ferocious warriors on earth.

There is another side to the samurai culture of Japan, however. As stated earlier the Japanese imported their higher culture from China, much as Westerners do from France. Chinese culture was derived from Confucianism, and, therefore, there was likewise a strong Confucian core to Japanese culture. The works of Mencius were used to train the young, and Confucianism formed the backdrop for the ethics of *bushido.*[235]

Confucianism in the context of *bushido*, however, did not mean intellectual specialization, but helped to develop an ethical "emotion."[236] The Japanese, very much like the Confucians themselves, saw the intellectual specialist as more akin to a machine than a human being.[237] To be human meant to subordinate the intellect to the feelings. Accordingly, the Japanese have a highly, almost morbidly developed "sense of shame" or *ren-chi-shin*.[238] To the Japanese, the sense of shame is the soil of all the virtues.[239]

Another aspect of the subordination of the intellect to one's feelings is that the samurai could be highly sentimental. The term *bushi no nasake* means the "tenderness of a warrior."[240] This goes far to explain the fascination of the samurai class with poetry and the custom of writing a quick "death poem" before going into battle. These poems were often found after battle stuffed into the breastplate or helmet of a fallen samurai.[241] Music, poetry, and dance were all studied by samurai youth specifically to cultivate the feelings of tenderness. This is the same culture that gave the world flower arranging and the kamikaze.

The Japanese emphasized the Confucian principle of righteousness or rectitude (*Yi*) and made it the cornerstone of the samurai ethic. *Gishi* indicates a "man of rectitude" and is the highest praise even during peacetime. *Gishi* is superior to any term that signifies mere mastery of an art or a technique, such as swordsmanship, archery, poetry, etc. *Gishi* is related to the spirit of the whole man and was derived from Mencius who had brought *Yi* or righteousness to the same level as *Jen* or love.[242] Perhaps the Japanese term involves both *Jen* and *Yi*. *Gishi* is, after all, motivated by *Jen* or love.[243]

If love is not enough to motivate one to act correctly, then reason must be used, and the concept of *giri* comes into play.[244] *Giri* literally means "right reason," and has come to denote duty or debt.[245] It is inferior to love and is called the secondary power of samurai ethics.[246] It was held that *giri* only became necessary when society became artificial and stratified,[247] that is, when it lost the initial family unity as preached under Shinto.

Giri eventually disintegrated into a justification for custom and a fear of censure. It became a vague sense of propriety.[248]

A more important aspect of the Confucian influence combined with the samurai spirit is the Japanese sense of courtesy and etiquette. The Confucians had stated that "benevolence is man."[249] The supreme virtues and the highest attributes of the human soul, for the Japanese, were love, magnanimity, sympathy, and pity.[250] This engendered a highly sensitive respect for the feelings of others.[251] Indeed, to this day if one goes to Japan, one will never hear a Japanese say "no." It is considered impolite as likely to hurt your feelings.[252] Since the highest form of politeness approaches the highest form of virtue, that is, love,[253] etiquette was highly developed in Japan.

For the Japanese, etiquette involves economy and grace. Grace is defined as the most economical manner of motion. There are no wasted gestures. An example, of course, is the *Cha-no-yu*, or the tea ceremony.[254] In our study of the work of Alexander Lowen, we have encountered this emphasis on grace. Gracefulness in activity is considered an indication that one's energy is flowing smoothly and one has no unresolved conflicts in one's mine or body. Gracefulness thus indicates overall health and is, therefore, compatible both with Chinese medicine and *Qi Gong*. Indeed, the Japanese concept of gracefulness and etiquette are specifically concerned with the storage and reserve of energy.[255] Fine manners are indicative of power in repose.[256] There is also a practical martial aspect to all of this. The Ogasawara School of Etiquette asserted that the end or purpose of all etiquette is to so cultivate oneself that even when one is quietly seated, no one, not even the coarsest thug, would dare to approach you.[257] They would viscerally feel your energy and power.

This may sound far-fetched, but as a prosecutor, my office has often been involved in victim training programs, and we teach people that the surest way to avoid being seen by an attacker as a victim is to appear calm and confident, to walk and act smoothly and relaxedly. This is grace, and it naturally implies power.

The author Inazo Nitobe', in his book, *Bushido the Soul of Japan*, flatly states that through the constant exercise of correct manners, one brings all of the faculties of one's mind and body into such order and harmony with both themselves and their environment as to indicate a final mastery of the spirit over the flesh.[258] The Japanese knight or samurai is, therefore, a combination of the ferociously loyal warrior skilled in all of the techniques of warfare, the Confucian gentleman, and the intense sensitivity of which only the Japanese are capable. The emphasis, however, is not on any one of these parts, mastery of which, by itself, is despised, but on the synthesis; the total human being: the samurai.

We have stated that there was an unwritten code of conduct for the samurai which joined them in class and united them in a shared ethical consciousness. An example of the way this code expressed itself is the *Hagakure* of Jocho Yamamoto. Jocho had been a samurai, and had literally had days where he had arrived at his evening prayers "splattered with blood after stepping over corpses all way."[259] When his lord and master died, Jocho had planned to commit seppuku, but had been forbidden to do so by his dying master. Instead, Jocho retired to a cottage in the woods and wrote his impressions of the samurai life. *Hagakure* literally means "hidden among the leaves."[260]

The relevance of *Hagakure* is not confined, however, to the bygone days of the samurai. It was read extensively by the Japanese during World War II and revived by the commentary of the internationally esteemed writer Yukio Mishima. Mishima's commentary, which was published after his public suicide in protest of the lack of the same traditional samurai values expressed in the *Hagakure,* became an instant best-seller in Japan after his death.[261]

Mishima begins his commentary with Jocho's central observation that the way of the samurai is death. Jocho further elaborates by asserting that in any situation where it is just as likely for one to die as to live one should "simply choose death."[262]

This attitude is appalling, quite incomprehensible, and

almost non-existent in the West — except for the Romans. The Romans, like the Japanese, were an imperial people who valued the epicurean pleasures of life, but who lived constantly in the shadow of death, either on the field or from one's own hand in the face of failure. But what kind of life can be derived from such a starting point?

First, the constant meditation on death emphasizes individualism. We face birth and death alone. Therefore, the Confucian goal of self-cultivation takes on an excruciatingly pleasurable intensity. It becomes important how one does something, not what effect one's actions will have, since one must assume as a warrior, that one will not be around to view the results.[263] Self-respect is, therefore, of paramount importance.[264]

Further, subjectivity becomes heightened under the ethics of the samurai.[265] Action, while action is possible, is valued. The individual samurai, and he alone, is able to choose and evaluate his own actions.[266] Death to Jocho and Mishima is the conclusion of all action.[267] This may sound bizarre, but it is not dissimilar to Sartre's position that as we make choices in life, we continually narrow the field of possible choices, until the final possibility, the final choice is made at the point of death. Life comes to a point. In fact, Mishima uses the image of a continually narrowing circle to illustrate the life of the samurai.[268] He contrasts this with the ever-expanding circles of the artists,[269] but I feel that this opposition is inapposite.

Mishima also argues that the realization of the nearness of death allows for freedom itself. Life is short and will end. One will never see the ultimate results of one's efforts. To live one's life doing things one does not want to do is, therefore, the height of stupidity.[270]

Finally, the samurai's consciousness of death makes love possible. When one knows that time is limited, one realizes one has to savor each minute. Accordingly, one develops a conscious sense of appreciation. One appreciates and values things. One loves. Love is valued so much precisely because of the intensity of the feelings it engenders. One is alive. One feels. This observation gives psychological insight into the intense sensitivity of the ferocious samurai warrior. Love, as we have shown in our discussion of bioenergetics, is intimately bound with what Reich called orgone, Freud and Jung, libido, and, the Chinese, *Qi*. To the Japanese, the word is *Ki*.

Love is valued by the samurai — as with the Western knight, as we shall see — since it causes energy to build and, therefore, permits the eventual utilization of such energy for the accomplishments of grand deeds.[271] To the samurai, as for the Western knight, the greatest love must be a secret love. The beloved's name should not even be uttered. The samurai must be prepared to die for love.[272]

This all sounds morbid but makes a great deal of bioenergetic sense in the context of a society engaged in constant warfare. To engage constantly in the strains of battle, especially battle involving heavy armor and iron weapons, one needs great reserves of energy. As we saw in our discussion of *Qi Gong*, nothing builds energy like erotic stimulation. Accordingly, if one were to ease the tension by actual physical release, one would be depleted. (Somehow I remember my high school football coach saying the same thing, but, it was a Catholic school after all, and perhaps football isn't on the same level as mortal combat.)

The free, overly subjective, constantly aroused individual that is produced by such an ethic is an odd duck indeed. Mishima emphasized his eccentricity and fanaticism,[273] and his worship of energy and passion.[274] Energy is good. Lethargy is bad. Action in the face of death is freedom, love, and a joy in itself.

Starting from this position, and the type of person it produces, Jocho has some interesting and entertaining observations derived from the Confucian spirit of *Bushido*. "Delicacy," that is, consideration for others, is a samurai precept. Again, tolerance for others is made possible by the knowledge of imminent death.[275] Righteousness or *Yi* itself is seen in this light as relative. Righteousness implies some sort of external standard, but that contradicts the samurai's sense of individuality, subjectivity, and freedom. Further, one cannot even die for a just cause since history is constantly re-evaluating the justness of all causes.[276] What is seen as just today, such as the settlement of the American frontier, will be seen as unjust tomorrow; consider the popularity of *Bury My Heart at Wounded Knee*. Since righteousness is both contradictory and relative, only the actions, the use of energy itself is pure. To die having failed in one's mission is to die like a fanatic, but, it is not dishonorable.[277] If one lives one's life ready to die, one cannot possibly make a mistaken or wrong action.[278] Use of energy is the motivating principle of action, and there can never be too much energy.[279] Once this is admitted, the person must simply follow the physical laws of energy.[280] However, while the samurai follows nature, he will never meet a natural death. His death, like his life, must be free. That is why Hara Kiri or self destruction is the ultimate expression of free will; the ultimate victory.[281]

Confucius advised that one must take small matters seriously.[282] Lord Naoshige, quoted by Jocho, urges one to take large matters lightly.[283] The moment is appreciated as an aesthetic experience. Therefore, the resolution of the moment is the only thing that matters.[284] In that moment, small things are taken seriously and weighty concerns, lightly.

Because time is so short, the samurai requires that each moment be beautiful. What is beautiful is defined as strong, vivid, and "brimming with energy."[285] A corollary to this is that what is moral must be beautiful,[286] and this is the very point that we have urged concerning ethics. Mishima in his commentary likens this samurai attitude to that of the ancient Greeks, who also associated ethics with aesthetics.[287] Since what is beautiful depends on its energy content, we are back to Reich, Lowen, and the *Qi Gong* masters.

As an example of this attitude towards aesthetics, Jocho recommends that the samurai use cosmetics.[288] Why? Because a samurai might be "run through" at any moment, and to appear unhealthy and poorly groomed when one died would make one's enemies laugh.[289]

Much of the foregoing, I must concede, seems patently silly if not downright insane. However, our attitude to these expressions of the samurai code is conditioned, I would argue, not by any innate foolishness or insanity in the code itself, but in our belief that we live in a safe and secure society. The samurai lived in a milieu in which he could literally be "run through at any moment." This knowledge dictates a certain style of life. It is not all that bizarre in the context of that life to be concerned with one's appearance in death, since death is an inevitable and possibly swift reality. The attitudes and behaviors of someone constantly facing death are very different from one who feels, or deludes him or herself into feeling, that he or she is safe and secure and death is far away.

Most of us do not go to our dinner tables literally "splattered with blood after having stepped over corpses all day." However, many of us do this figuratively more often than we may want to admit. We are dissatisfied. We are in a constant state of stress and tension. We differ from the samurai and his ever-present make-up kit only in that he recognizes the source of his outlook and acts accordingly. The basic Buddhist insight that partly informs the samurai code, that all life is suffering or conflict, is valid for all of us. If we recognize this, our attitude changes. One who constantly faces great peril will become inordinately fixated on the moments he or she has. They are all one has and can be sure of. Their every action, therefore, has great meaning and intensity. This concentration on behavior is the essence of ethics. Ethics is nearly impossible in an overly comfortable society. Where there is abundance, there is waste. The biggest waste is the waste of time. Time is the ground of being and of ethics. The one thing that the professional warrior cannot waste is time. Ethics, therefore, does not come from the priestly caste of society, which is after all mainly concerned with the placating and pacification of an external being according to external rules; but from the class of warriors. Ethics is individual, subjective, aesthetic, and a matter of free choice. It is the free production and use of energy.

Lest one thinks that all of this is simply confined to the Asian psyche, the parallels with European chivalry are instructive, and did not go unnoticed by the Japanese authors cited above. Both Nitobe' and Mishima make comparisons between the samurai knights of Japan and the medieval knights of Europe.[290] The profession and its concentration on its behavior are quite similar.

In the West the concept of chivalry, the European equivalent of *Bushido*, also first developed in the Twelfth Century.[291] Prior to that time, when referring to armed fighting men, the terms used were *bellatores,* or *pugnatores,* which meant warriors rather than knights[292] and was thus more akin to the term *bushi* as opposed to "samurai."

In 1170, Etienne de Fougeres, Bishop of Liseaux, used the word *chevelerie* to denote the code of a separate class, the mounted knight.[293] *Chevelerie* is derived from the French word *cheval* or horse.[294] Accordingly, chivalry is the code of the mounted knight. The spirit of the code of the Western mounted knight, the *chevalier,* or cavalier, is as different from the Japan of the samurai as Western religion is from Eastern. In the West, while the orders of chivalry were largely secular, there was an admixture of Christian religion and clerical participation in the ritual and philosophy of chivalry.[295] Since most, if not all books were written by Christian monks, naturally the highest duty of the Christian knight was to protect the Christian faith.[296] Without the admixture of the clerical learning, however, the orders of chivalry would have meant nothing more than an hereditary military professionalism.[297] This would be equivalent to the "mere technician" so despised by Jocho. Instead, with the spiritual influence of Christianity, the whole man was to be developed; his spirit as well as his military and physical skills.[298] Again, this is very much like the concept of the samurai put forward by Jocho, Mishima, and Nitobe.

It is to be emphasized, however, that while the Christian church influenced and provided the ideals for the orders of chivalry, the orders themselves were basically secular, with a class consciousness of their own, and free of priestly control. These fighting men were also more humanistically oriented and less abstract in their outlook than the clergy.[299] This would naturally follow from the fact of combat which, after all, involved man against man.

Eventually secular authors attempted to provide guidelines for the knights of Christendom. Two such men were

Geoffry de Charny and Ramon Lull.[300] Though we will discuss Lull's work in more detail below, the important point to remember is that while European chivalry was steeped in Christianity and freely used Christian images, its class consciousness and the technical and existential realities of the profession of arms made it as much akin to the Japanese samurai as to the church militant. Fighting is fighting. Facing imminent death is the same for a Japanese as it is for a Frenchman. The consciousness and philosophy developed from the realities of constant warfare are essentially the same.

The knightly qualities were five in number: *Prouesse* (prowess), *Loyaute* (loyalty), *Largesse* (generosity), *Courtoisie* (courtesy), and *Franchise* (a free and confident bearing which is the visible sign of the combination of good birth and virtue).[301] It is quite obvious that these are qualities that are equally present and valued by the samurai ethic. Only *largesse* needs a word of explanation.

In the Eleventh Century, a technical innovation radically changed the style of warfare in the West. The stirrup permitted a mounted knight to use the "couched" lance.[302] The couched lance was held under the arm and braced so that it could be driven at the enemy in a cavalry charge. Prior to that time, mounted knights had used spears very much like foot soldiers. Now, the stirrup made the massed cavalry charge the essence of medieval battles.[303]

The problem was that these innovations caused the knight using and exposed to such crushing lance charges to require heavier and stronger horses and heavier and stronger armor. Lances also had a bad habit of breaking. All of this was expensive.[304] It was suddenly not as easy for the poorer knights to arm themselves. The continual cost of horses and armor would break a knight's estate.[305] Therefore, the poorer knights looked to their lords and richer brethren for the distribution of spoils and other financial benefits acquired in battle.[306] A generous lord was, accordingly, highly honored.[307]

Like the samurai, the knight was honored for his virtues, and not simply for technical skill. The European knights were ranked by Charny accordingly. A good, simple, and bold knight was called *preux*. Those who by valor are raised to a higher rank are *soulverain preux*. But those who are *plus soulverain preux* have the wisdom to see the hand of God and the Virgin in their endeavors.[308]

Unlike the Japanese, the Christian knight had the concept of the "just war." His Bible, especially the *Old Testament*, gave him examples of this and, after the victory of the Christian Emperor Constantine, gave it a Christian example, St. Augustine of Hippo developed the theory of the just war that was passed on to the medieval West.[309] It was the basis of the Crusades, and Pope Urban I in his sermon at Clermont in which he launched the First Crusade, promised that those who fought would be granted the remission of all penance for their sins.[310] Since the knight was judged by his valor, the Western warrior class searched for wars in which to fight. The Crusades gave them both worldly and religious advantages, as did the wars against the Moslems in Spain and, later, the Crusades into pagan Poland and Lithuania by the Teutonic Knights.[311]

A seasoned fighter was highly valued and if, in the unlikely prospect one could not readily find a war to gain honors, there was always the tournament.

Tournaments were originally nearly indistinguishable from real battles.[312] They generally took place between "teams" of knights, usually between villages with no referees, no sidelines, and very sharp, very real weapons.[313] At the infamous tournament of Neuss in 1241, eighty knights were killed, most of them suffocating in their armor after being unhorsed.[314] The tournaments were strongly condemned by the Church and Christian burial forbidden to anyone falling in a tournament.[315] Nevertheless, the martial calling led knights from all over Christendom to disobey the Church.[316]

Part of the basis of both warfare and the tournament was the idea of courtly love.[317] Again, we see the parallel with the Japanese samurai class, and like that class, the function of love was not physical consummation, but to drive the knights to greater feats of strength and daring.[318]

As the Western knights became more and more conscious of themselves as a distinct group, they looked to express themselves and their deeds in writing as examples of valor and virtue, for both training and entertainment.[319] The troubadours put the knightly exploits into verse, drawing from the classical histories of Greece and Rome, and from the Celtic stories surrounding one Arthur Pendragon, better known as King Arthur.[320]

Eventually these stories developed into the cult of the "Nine Worthies" as embodying examples for the knights of the present day. The Nine Worthies are as follows: From the *Old Testament*: Joshua, David, and Judas Macabeus. From the Classical world: Hector, Alexander the Great, and Julius Caesar. From the Christian world: Arthur, Charlemagne, and Geoffry de Bouillon.[321] Geoffry may be unfamiliar to many readers. He was the Christian liberator of Jerusalem during the First Crusade and was believed to have been prefigured by Alexander as a European conqueror of the East.[322]

The development of massed archers and then of gunpowder spelled the end of the armored knight as the epitome of the fighting man.[323] The advent of these weapons called for heavier and prohibitively expensive plate armor, and many noble families simply did not have the means to continue to serve the martial functions that they had performed during the heyday of chivalry.[324] Nonetheless, the ideals of courage, generosity, and courtly love continued in the West long after the effectiveness of the mounted warrior was eclipsed by massed infantry and artillery.

At the end of the Middle Ages, chivalry became much more closely associated with the nobility.[325] As modern armies were being formed, the new officer class was accordingly drawn from the old nobility.[326] The ideals of the orders of chivalry thus continued until the advent of universal conscription during the French Revolution. One officer of the old school complained upon facing the new conscripted French Revolutionary Army that the French won by cheating. Their men hated his men. That was no way for a soldier to behave![327]

As with the East, the European code of chivalry was unwritten and casuistic. Nonetheless, as with Jocho

Yamamoto's *Hagakure,* similar treatises derived from the principles of chivalry and attempting to give guidance to the warriors of the time also appeared in Europe. Perhaps the most influential of these was the *Book of the Orders of Chivalry* by Ramon Lull.[328] Lull's book served as the handbook of chivalric values in all of the countries of Europe except for Germany,[329] whose system of knighthood was different from that of the French from which Lull would have been influenced.[330]

Lull lived from 1232-1316 and began his career as a *seneschal* at the Court of King James II of Aragon. A *seneschal* has charge of the king's domestic arrangements and servants.[331] After service as a fighting knight and courtier, Lull had a vision of Christ and renounced warfare in favor of missionary work among the Moslems of North Africa. He was martyred by being stoned to death in Tunis when he was in his eighties.[332] In addition to being a knight, Lull was a poet, mystic, occultist, philosopher, and alchemist.[333]

Lull's book on chivalry begins, as does the *Hagakure,* with an old knight who has retired to the woods so that he will not bring dishonor to his profession because of the feebleness of old age.[334] After praying to God and thanking him for the many honors of his military career,[335] he encounters a squire who has wandered off the path in the forest while on his way to be dubbed a knight.[336] The book consists of the advice the aged knight gives to the youth concerning the life and values of a knight.[337]

Lull's knight begins by explaining to the squire that chivalry gives the knight his whole identity.[338] Fear of injustice originally caused the people to pick one man out of a thousand to protect them and to enforce justice. That man was picked for his loyalty, strength, courage, breeding, and manners.[339] The knight used the horse since the horse was the strongest and most noble of animals.[340]

The knight, the squire was told, must be both loved and feared. Loved because he upholds charity and instruction in religion, and the virtues. Feared because he enforces justice and truth.[341] Because of his honors in this life, the knight, Lull taught, was held to a higher standard by God.[342] A knight has grave responsibilities and duties. If he does not perform them he is not a knight. In fact, he is to be despised as less than the most common serf who does his duties in the fields.[343] The knight has the duties to protect and defend the other members of society, especially women, children, widows, and the elderly, to spread the Christian faith and, to support and defend his earthly lord and his native land.[344]

Lull, like Jocho, also makes the central and defining assertion that the knight, like the samurai, must embody not only physical strength, but the moral virtues. In the West, those knightly virtues were: justice, wisdom, charity, loyalty, truth, humility, strength, hope, and promptness.[345] Also like Jocho, Lull plainly states that the inner virtues are more important than technical skills or physical strength. To bolster this assertion, however, Lull uses a typically Western argument, that being that the soul is more excellent than the body, therefore, inner virtue is more excellent than mere physical skill or strength.[346] Lull adds that the less impressive a knight's arms, the less help that he receives from others, the more the true knight must rely on his own inner strength and courage, and if he, like his samurai brethren, should die in such a situation, he is remembered as having permanently possessed these virtues.[347]

Two of the virtues listed by Lull require special attention. Humility is a particularly Christian addition to the virtues. No Western pagan culture, such as the Greeks or Romans, had any concept of humility. As pointed out by Nietzsche, these aristocratic cultures divided the world into good and bad. To be poor, weak, and sickly was bad. It was natural for the strong, rich, and healthy to despise the others and not feel in any way out of line for doing so. With the advent of Christianity, again as demonstrated by Nietzsche, these values were stood on their head. The rich, powerful, and strong were now to serve the poor and weak.

Hope is the other virtue that needs a word of explanation. Here we have an apparent departure from the thought of Jocho, who flatly states that the warrior should choose an honorable death and be unconcerned with the outcome of his endeavors since they are all relative. The Western knight, however, possesses the specifically Christian virtue of hope.

Hope, according to Lull, is the principal instrument of the
knight. Without hope, the knight would not have the power
to do his job.[348] Hope gives the knight the courage to believe
that he will be victorious no matter what the odds.[349] This
concern with victory seems to be at odds with Jocho's
advice to disregard such thoughts. However, are the two
positions really so different?

Victory can be defined in many ways. The ultimate victory for the Christian was resurrection and union with God
after death. Accordingly, a Christian knight slain in a battle in
which he believed he was fighting in a just cause was
assured of heaven. Therefore, he was assured of ultimate victory even though he would die. Given this insight, would
there be a great deal of difference in facing either a determined samurai or a Christian knight convinced that he was
engaged in a just fight? Both would fight fanatically to the
death. It was their way of life.

One further note on hope. Hope is one of the theological
virtues.[350] It is particularly associated with the Holy Spirit in
the Christian religion. When the Spirit came upon the disciples of Christ on Pentecost, it was felt as a surge of great
power. Except for the source, which the Christian believer
asserts is directly from God, is the phenomenological effect
of this internal power any different from the power derived
from prolonged *Qi Gong* practice? The descent of the Spirit
on Pentecost was accompanied by a roaring of wind and was
seen as tongues of fire.[351] Prolonged and advanced *Qi Gong*
practice also is accompanied by such phenomenon. This is
not the place to go into all of this, but the reader is advised
to consult Dr. Yang Jwing-Ming's seminal work on *Qi Gong*,
The Root of Chinese Chi Kung, especially pages 176-178. The
point is that the emphasis in the West, as in the East, is on
internal virtue. Virtue as we have seen denotes a form of biological energy and potency. Although the belief systems and
language used to describe this internal energy phenomenon
may differ, having a Taoist or Buddhist vocabulary in the
East, and a Christian, Pentecostal one in the West, the bioenergetic insight remains the same.

This position is further borne out by the place of love in chivalry. Courtly love is an integral part of chivalry. Charny stated plainly that the knight should be in love.[352] *Par armours*. Love of a great lady leads the knight to great feats of valor and strength — just as prescribed by Jocho for his samurai.

The connection with bioenergetic power is further emphasized by the fact that the dubbing ceremony for knights was, according to Lull, ideally to be performed on Christmas, Easter, or Pentecost.[353] The ceremony was performed by a presiding knight and a priest.[354] Every item of the knight's equipage had a mystical meaning, such as the sword for justice, spear for truth, helmet for fear of shame, and the miserecord, or narrow dagger, for trust in God, not in heavy weapons.[355] The ethos of chivalry was brought together finally in the image of St. George and the dragon. This is really a rehash in Christian garb of Perseus and the Sea Monster, but the fact that this pagan story was important enough to be adopted by Christian culture says much for the strength of its insight. St. George rescues the maiden from the dragon. He uses all of the mystically symbolic weapons of chivalry — weapons that represent the virtues. Here we have the chivalric ideal of the love of a lady spurring the knight to higher achievement. Here we have the alchemical transformation and sublimation of the biosexual energy, represented in the West, as in the East, by the dragon, and the triumph of the Christian knight armed with the Christian virtues.

Lull's book, like Jocho's, is important not because of any rules which it may impose, since neither book does that, but because it embodies the attitudes of the warrior class it serves to guide. In both, the central principle is that the total person is to be considered and that a strong and skillful fighter without the inner virtues is not a person worthy of the title of knight or samurai. Lull, as well as the Lord of Mito, quoted by Nitobe, points out that even robbers and brigands can be fierce fighters.[356] Nor is intelligence and learning enough. Lull argues that intelligence is necessary,[357] but as Jocho asserts, a scholar without virtue is simply a machine and even merchants are very intelligent in their own fields.[358] The sense of virtue is the sine qua non of both the samurai and the knight. It is inner strength or virtue that makes one a member of the warrior elite.

But living by this inner strength leads to a certain outlook on life, as demonstrated above. The virtuous person is different from the run of humankind. The person with a martial outlook proceeds differently, from a different perspective, than other people.

In 1603 Tokugawa Ieyasu established the Tokugawa *bakufu* or military government for Japan, and internal warfare ceased to be a dominant feature of Japanese life. During this era, the Edo period, which lasted from 1603-1868, ending with the Meiji Restoration, the samurai families lost their military effectiveness and the Japanese people lived in a social straight-jacket.[359] The Tokugawas discouraged military training except in a traditional, almost ceremonial manner.[360] Additionally, as in the West, conscript armies, using firearms, were easily able to slaughter the traditionally armed warriors of the samurai class.[361]

The Tokugawas preferred to divert the energies of the people, especially those who could resist their dictatorship, to non-martial pursuits. Accordingly, the Neo-Confucianism of Chu Hsi, with its idealization of the past and emphasis on literature and etiquette as opposed to martial pursuits, was imported from China.[362] Confucianism, as we have seen, however, is a broad system and includes many points of view. The Japanese people, while outwardly required to conform to the rigid structures of the *Shogunate,* sought, as to do all human beings, freedom of thought and expression. This, of course, is because freedom is the nature of human beings, as we have seen in our earlier discussion of human nature.

The Confucian interpretation of Wang Yang-Ming attracted the attention of the literate Japanese.[363] Wang's system, called *Oyomei* in Japanese, was completely personal and individual and stressed reliance on one's intuition and virtue rather than on one's intellect. *Oyomei* asserted that it is in dedication to physical action that one learns to control one's mind and to "exemplify illustrious virtue."[364] A unity of knowledge and action is developed through self-discipline, and through such physical discipline a human being can learn to achieve the goal of Confucian philosophy; self-cultivation and self-perfection.[365] Wang valued action over words and urged men and women to assert themselves and improve their own lives.[366] He favored individual merit over heredity privilege and military dictatorship.[367] The philosophy of Wang, the *Oyomei,* was severely criticized by the Tokugawa *Shogunate,* and the most specific of the criticisms leveled against Wang was that he was much too interested in martial strategy and tactics. This was not the sort of thing the Tokugawas wanted to be the concern of their "gentlemen."[368]

By the time that the Tokugawas imported the Neo-Confucianism of the Chu Hsi, they could not help but bring in the elements of Taoism that had become part of the Neo-Confucian system. As we know from our discussion of Taoism, it is a highly individualistic philosophy, and gives a person the impetus to look beyond conventional values and mores to what is truly beyond language and thought. Taoism, with its emphasis on longevity, medicine, and the martial arts, also encouraged the Japanese to find wisdom in the unity of action and knowledge through physical endeavor.[369]

Orthodox Taoism viewed the Tao as an abstract, almost contentless term describing something beyond all concepts. The Japanese, however, were less apt to adopt this type of intellectual view, and changed its meaning to the more earthly "way" or "path." The Japanese word for Tao is *do*.[370]

The Japanese concept of a *do* is that of a long, arduous road filled with many difficulties, tests, and challenges, leading eventually to self-perfection. The road *itself*, the *do*, is the path of self-cultivation.[371]

A *do* is not a religion, although it rests on a spiritual foundation. Spirituality is the motivating factor and background of a do, but there is no superstition or worship involved.[372] A *do* is essentially action. As action, constant training is involved. This training is the way. Constant physical training was believed to build character. Character, virtue, was the basis of all man-made systems.[373] Without character and virtue, the Japanese believed that no man-made system could work. It is too obvious, of course, to point to our own present society in the United States as an example of the results of a breakdown in moral character. Even in a benevolent democracy with extensive physical comforts and economic opportunities, without a basic training in character and self-cultivation, the system breaks down.

Nor will physical training itself develop the type of person envisioned by the *do* masters. We are also all too aware of the failings of our professional and amateur athletes. In the *do* forms, there is a mental element. Intuition and wisdom are sought. Philosophically, the goal of the *do* forms is to understand the whole of life through a tiny segment of it.[374]

This brings us to the relationship of *do* and Zen. Zen, like all forms of Buddhist practice, aims at enlightenment and liberation. This is not the place for a lengthy discussion of Buddhism, but the greatest obstacle to enlightenment is self-deception.[375] The physical forms of the *do* are utilized to prevent self-deception.

In traditional Zen, one meditates for hours on end. I, while not a regular practitioner of Zen, have participated in this type of practice. One sits and basically goes nuts with boredom. However, after a while an odd thing happens; the mind slows down and shuts off. I do not claim any form of enlightenment for myself, but I can see that when this mind-freeze occurs, one is at least open. From this state one can proceed to allow the true mind, the intuitive, to emerge. Buddhist philosophy teaches that the ultimate deception is the erroneous belief in an individual "I," or self. Clinging to this belief, one is attracted to things that make the "I" feel good, and one avoids those things that do not support the "I." By eliminating these erroneous beliefs and self-created deceptions, one becomes free. Freedom, again, is the essence of the human being. To be free and open allows one to act without baggage. This unleashes great power and vision. The method of the *do* forms, like Zen meditation or Zen koans, forces the mind to shut down and allows the power to emerge.

Again with Zen we return to the idea of energy. Chinese alchemy, which is derived from *Qi Gong* practice, depends on the direction of massive amounts of *Qi* (*Ki* — Japanese) into the mystical "gates" or channels of the *Qi* field in order to open an energy flow into the practitioner's spiritual body. This can take an amount of energy at least ten times greater than normally produced by the body. Zen also depends on this type of massive accumulation of energy. It is to be remembered that Zen originated in China where it was called *Ch'an.*

In order to gain enlightenment and freedom, energy must be withdrawn from its absorption in the physical and mental "chatter" of everyday life. The twitches, fidgeting, daydreams, worries, etc., must be shut down so that energy can be collected. Unlike alchemy, however, in which the goal is the creation of a spiritual body and in which therefore, conscious direction of energy is possible, Zen is concerned with liberation. It uses its accumulated energy to produce an atomic blast which propels its practitioner beyond all concepts, images, and delusions, including the ultimate delusion — self-delusion. The Zen practitioner creates a "short-circuit."

The techniques used to create this short-circuit include meditation and the *koan.* The *koan* is a nonsense question that is put to the practitioner by his or her master. It has no discursive answer and is intended to confuse and "fuse" all of the mental circuits. When the practitioner has melted as much of his or her mind as possible with a *koan,* another is given. There is no end until the mind explodes.

In the *do* forms, *kata* serves the function of the *koan* in sitting practice. *Kata* are exercises, "forms," that progressively integrate the techniques of a *do* discipline. Like the *koan,* they are repeated ad nauseam until the mind, the body, and the *kata* fuse. Even that is not enough. At first, all of one's energy is taken up in just learning and performing the physical movements. Eventually, as the *kata* becomes perfected, energy is freed. The mind concentrates on the *kata* and energy is not absorbed by the scattered twitchings of the mind-body continuum. The sensei may try to confuse the student. He or she may change an element of the *kata*. He or she may purposely make a "mistake." The student must adjust intuitively.

Again, as the *kata* is learned, energy freed, and mind frozen, new *katas* are practiced until one becomes the *do*. One acts without effort or discursive thought. One is the *do*. One no longer needs the techniques or the methods. One is the spirit of these things. In Buddhist thought there is the image of a boat and a river. One needs the boat to cross the river, but once the river is crossed, the boat can be discarded. That is the same as the practice of a *do*.

Why *budo*, however? Why did the Japanese develop their *do* from martial pursuits? In truth, any activity would do for a *do*; flower arranging, serving tea, writing poetry. But the arts of war are nearer in many ways to the Japanese spirit and to the spirit of Buddhism. The Japanese people had been engaged in warfare for eight hundred years. Martial techniques were an integral part of their consciousness. Further, the samurai's continual existence under the shadow of death was an apropos metaphor for the devout Buddhist. We are all under the shadow of death. Constant exposure to martial training is a continual reminder of that fact, and puts one in a frame of mind receptive to religious concerns. The martial philosophy, such as that of the *Hagakure*, if transposed into the battle of everyday life, gives the *budo* practitioner a mindset that is more conscious, intentional, and rich than that of the everyday, semi-conscious or unconscious life of the majority of people. Just to continually recall that the way of the samurai is death, and, that one should act purely and decisively since the results of one's action are ultimately unknowable, deepens one's appreciation of everyday life. Just as with the medieval samurai, this consciousness permits one to act freely and tolerantly. Compassionately, in Buddhist terms.

The object of the martial training in *budo*, however, is different from *bushido*. The *bushi* trained for warfare to defeat of an enemy. The practitioner of *budo* trains to conquer him or herself.[376] Self-delusion is to be destroyed. Like the

Christian knight whose weapons were actually seen as symbols of his religious consciousness, so too the "weapons" of the *budoka*.

From the foregoing discussion of *bushido*, chivalry, and *budo*, it must be apparent that while virtue and virtuous conduct were valued, there are no "rules" per se. The only "rules" of conduct come from the internal promptings of the physical energy or *Qi* of the samurai, knight, or *budoka*. That the eventual "results" of these internal promptings fall within a range and are more often than not similar, only indicate that they follow the same natural laws of bioenergy. This does not in any way negate the inherent individualism of the practitioner as emphasized by Jocho and Mishima. The individual remains free, and, is in fact, freer than the run of humanity because his or her goal is self-cultivation or perfection. The individual seeking self-cultivation is existentially free simply, as our study has shown, by being human. However, the material with which he or she works as a *budoka* is the bioenergy or *Qi* of his or her own energy field. *Qi* is the medium of expression. Properly handled, it gives strength or virtue, and, clarity and transcendence. Nor does the fact that one trains extensively in a *do* form indicate a lack of consciousness like that exhibited by the church lady. Instead, one is consciously directing the only medium that truly grounds and spontaneously produces virtuous behavior; one's internal power or energy.

Life, as the Buddhist insight explains, is struggle. What more appropriate model exists for meeting the adversity which is the essence of life than that of martial training? However, while life and death situations do occur in our lives more often than we wish to admit, most of our time is spent in more peaceful struggles. It is unrealistic and irresponsible for us to go about heavily armed and disporting the morbid sense of honor of the samurai. However, it is not out of line for us to remember our place in the universe and to act with a full and deep understanding of our existential situation. *Budo*, by using martial forms and philosophy, constantly reminds us of our true place and provides the only realistic means of meeting the constant battles of everyday life; espe-

cially the most continuous and unrelenting of all battles —
the one against ourselves.

While all of us struggle, nowhere is the nature of adversity and the expectations higher for meeting that adversity than in the professions. In the final chapter we will apply the *budo* model to professional life. If one sees the challenges and confrontations of professional life as contests with oneself, then these struggles become *koans* and professional life, a *do*. As with all *dos*, one works to increase and direct one's energy so that one may enhance one's intuition and become a master. Not as a technician, but as a whole person. The only mastery is mastery of life.

CHAPTER FIVE

Ethics: Personal and Professional

In 1793, the town of Pizzighetone was besieged. During the siege, a bridge was thrown over the breach and tables were set. The officers of both the besieged and the besiegers entertained each other with balls, entertainments, and concerts. People flocked from the surrounding areas to what actually had all the trappings of a fair. It was described as "a delightful rendezvous."[377]

This is how the warfare of the Eighteenth Century was conducted. The armies of the absolute monarchs were professional standing armies and warfare was decidedly limited. Indeed, so professional and limited had warfare become, that Lawrence Sterne, an English citizen, traveled to France during the Seven Years War, forgot his passport, but was admitted to the country and traveled without incident, eventually receiving his passport from the French Foreign Minister as a courtesy. Eventually Sterne divided his time between his French admirers and the unmolested English expatriate colony at Frontignac. There was simply no evidence to indicate that the two countries were at war and Mr. Sterne quite honestly recorded "... it never entered my mind that we were at war with France."[378]

War between professionals is a different matter than a brawl among amateurs. Professionals are highly trained, not only in technical skills but, hopefully, also in a professional attitude. A professional, no matter where their ranking in the pecking order, is always armed. A professional knows how and when to use those arms.

There is a precept among Japanese swordsmen: If you

are better than your opponent, he will die. If he is better than you, you will die. If you are equally matched, you both will die. You, therefore, have two chances out of three to die. To this I add, do you really want to know who the best swordsman is in Japan?

My docket partner in the Prosecutor's Office once sat across from an equally experienced and equally skillful attorney from the Public Defender's Office. They were friends and had known each other for a long time. They were haggling over a plea bargain. In exasperation my partner asked, "Why should I give you a deal? Why shouldn't I just take this to trial?" To which his friend replied, "Because win or lose I can give you a miserable day." They struck a deal. Fights between professionals are not taken lightly, because once engaged, no quarter is given. Everybody knows this. That is what separates the professional from the non-professional. The professional knows what to expect.

There are four professions: medicine, the law, the ministry, and the military.[379] All professions are about fighting. The doctor fights illness and injury; the military man, the enemy; the minister, the powers of darkness; and, the lawyer, damn near everybody. That is why training should never be merely in technique. Nor, in reality, does that often happen. If one escapes his or her professional school with nothing more than technique, most times the real world practice of one's art will force one to develop an attitude as a professional person.

Originally, all professionals, except perhaps those in the military, were priests. Priests studied medicine, law, and theology as part of their training.[380] Since the professional was a priest, he received his sustenance from the Church. He was not paid by his patient or client. Over time, however, it became customary to "tip" the professional for a good job.[381] This "tip" became the professional's fee.[382] I have been in private legal practice, and some of my clients still confuse me with a priest!

The derivation of the professions from the priesthood is an interesting thing. The education of priests is seen as a matter of detached learning and contemplation. One looks above and beyond the affairs of the everyday, mundane world. Professionals in many ways are similarly trained. The first year of law school, as undoubtedly the first year of medical school, one might as well be in a monastery. Contact is broken with your former life, indeed, with any life, due to the overwhelming burden of the work assigned. It is like a cult. In many ways it is a form of brainwashing. By the end of the first semester, if you survive the exams, you can't conceive of life outside of law or medicine. By the end of the first year, by the time you are in that first clerkship or internship, you have become identified with your chosen profession. You will never be the same person again.

Do you know what I like about being a professional? When someone asks me what I do I can answer in three words: I'm a lawyer. No further explanation of my job is needed. When a non-professional is asked what they do, they must go into a description. The typical answer goes something like this: I work for Bozo Company in accounts receivable, or, I'm a marketing rep for Baboon Securities. The professional *is*. I *am* a doctor. I am a lawyer. Even if I work for somebody else, that is not my identity. Whether I work for a Fortune 500 company, or hang out my shingle, I *am* a lawyer. The professional has a sense of identity. A class consciousness, if you will.

During the Vietnam War, my father, a football coach, was a hawk. He continually derided all of the anti-war leaders he saw on the news — except for William Sloane Coffin. Why? Coffin had been an All-American football player. He belonged to my father's club. All my father could do was mutter to himself, "I can't understand that Coffin, he was an All-American." Like it or not, the respect had to be there. Professionals must and do feel the same way. You make it through law school or med school and actively practice, you deserve at least a minimum of respect.

At this point, a question needs to be raised concerning professional management. Can those who have trained to lead corporations or establish business enterprises be considered "professionals"? Militating against such a position is the fact that there is neither licensing nor a code of ethics or professional responsibility for business people. If I violate my code of professional responsibility, I can be disbarred. A priest or a minister can be defrocked. A doctor can lose his license to practice medicine. A business person engaging in unethical practices receives no such *professional* sanction. He or she faces no board of their peers. At most, the sanctions of the civil or the criminal law are applicable, but such general sanctions are applicable to everyone. No special group oversees the activities of the executive or the manager. The only possible exception to this is securities dealers who are tightly regulated and at least have some rudimentary principles of ethics concerning the types of people and types of investments that they work with.

In Japan, executives and even lower-level managers have a sense of responsibility not only to their enterprises, but to society at large. They are also intimately bound to the government of the country. In this sense, perhaps they are more "professional" than their American counterparts.

I don't mean to unduly slam American business people. After all, many lawyers, doctors, and even ministers are only in it for the money. I have an MBA and the training is oriented towards producing professional managers. I have done sales and marketing professionally and can easily make the argument that sales at least is just as difficult and requires just as much preparation as any trial work I've ever done. However, unlike the other professions mentioned, business is an unbroken continuum. There is simply no way to distinguish the professional from the amateur.

Nonetheless, I think it is unrealistic to exclude professional management from the ranks of the professions in a society such as ours. Too many people take the advanced training in management, and then "practice" their calling professionally during their lifetimes to be excluded. Their decisions affect far too many people so that the weight of responsibility is there for them if they choose to see it. Unfortunately, in America the bottom line is placed first. In Japan, the responsibility for one's employees and customers is a more integral part of the calculation of success. Historically, both the samurai and the knight had a responsibility to look after the material well-being of their dependents. In the West, additionally, there were religious and spiritual underpinnings to business practice. From Protestantism comes the idea that hard work and the resulting wealth are a gift from God showing his favor. From Catholicism comes the idea of the fair price and the fair day's wage. Judaism gives us the concept of philanthropy. Whether accepted or not by management then, social and professional responsibility remain bound with their calling, if only in principle.

We have our group then. Doctors, lawyers, clergymen, the military, and management are the professionals of our society. But before we discuss professional life and ethics, we should summarize what we have gleaned in our study of human being, virtue, and the martial arts model of life.

In our discussion of human being, which I will not reproduce here, we came to a number of conclusions. We found that while the human being has a physical body and could therefore be treated as a thing, he or she also transcends that body and possesses a part of being that is essentially free. This part of the person stands above "things" and has the power to interact with them and change them. This power to produce change is energy. In China, this energy is called *Qi*, and its quality, quantity, purity, and level in a human being are largely determinate of the type of human being a person is. However, *Qi*, being a "physical" concept, it is not wholly determinative of the human being since this would contradict the basic essence of human being, which is freedom. The free human person, while determined at one moment by his or her *Qi*, still has the freedom to manipulate that very *Qi*. *Qi Gong* is the practice of increasing, balancing, and directing the *Qi* flow in the human being. Through long and continuous practice, one can change the composition and direction of one's *Qi*, thereby altering the type of person one is. *Qi* is thus the medium of the human being.

Qi, which composes the human being, is energy. Energy is associated with power, and, power and energy are the basis of virtue. Virtue is a biologically derived term meaning strength and potency. Specifically the term has sexual overtones which comport with the insights of Chinese medicine, Western depth psychology, and classical philology.

What all of this means is that the human being, as a basically sexual being, is composed of energy. By being composed of energy, he or she possesses virtue or potency. Thus, as Mencius observed, all men and women are born good in the sense of having the beginnings of virtue. Left to our own nature, as the Chinese sages repeatedly asserted, we would develop the virtues and act in a manner that would express love and righteousness. This, also by the way, is the position of Reich and those following his bioenergetic theories.

Unfortunately, environment has a great deal to do with how the energy of human beings in a given society is expressed. According to classical philosophy, both Eastern and Western, society exists so that the happiness of the citizens can be maximized. Confucius, and one might add, Aristotle and the Christian philosophers, believed that society came into existence because the human is a social animal, that is, his or her basic instinct was to express love and attraction for fellow human beings. Therefore, he or she naturally forms relationships. Society and, eventually government and other organizations, commercial and fraternal, exist as a result of this human need. Government ideally exists, in this context, as a teaching entity. It is to guide and help the citizen in his or her pursuit of happiness. It was the insight of both Mencius and the Taoists, and, Wilhelm Reich that societies and governments often fail in their tasks with devastating effects on the individual. Accordingly, while the ideal would be a society and institutions that maximize the virtue in human beings, the reality, as realized by the Taoists, and, eventually by Reich, is that a person can ultimately only be responsible for his or her own virtue.

In many ways it would be nice if some external source could definitively provide the rules or instructions which, if followed, would lead to virtuous behavior and human happiness. Unfortunately this is a contradictory idea. In other words, due to the essence of human beings as free, and, one might add as a corollary to freedom, naturally creative, external compulsion is inhuman and, therefore, no human expression such as art or ethics can be based upon it. There can be no rules. If we start from this position, we will be on firm ground.

But we cannot simply allow things to just flow unregulated, can we? Unfortunately, since the physical dominance of males and the creation of the idea of property, our institutions have had to become more removed from nature and more intrusive in our lives. They have set an unnatural and mainly evil example, and we have been taught to need regulation. However, as with Tokugawa Japan, we can as individuals, maximize our own virtue and freedom. The question then before us is how to do this.

Our answer comes from the martial arts. It is true that we live in a society that is generally speaking, at peace. There is no need for us to go about armed to the teeth, and, unlike the situation during World War II, the vast majority of us are not and will not be soldiers. However, as most of the world's religions, and most notably Buddhism, observe, all life is struggle and conflict. The greatest conflict is within ourselves. This is especially true in a time when the government, our institutions, and those who we laughingly refer to as our leaders (of whatever political persuasion) cannot be trusted and are inured to rational dialogue.

This was precisely the situation that existed as *bushido* developed into *budo*. *Budo* used the martial philosophy and outlook of the warrior, the samurai or knight, to develop the inner strength and self-expression of the individual. The *do* forms, with their *kata*, became detached from their earlier, practical purposes, and were used as an avenue for the continuing self-cultivation of the individual.

The professional, like the knight or the samurai, stands in a special place in society. He or she, as pointed out by Mishima in his discussion of the samurai, is by nature an individual. Like the knight or samurai who, while essentially a free agent, gave fealty to a lord, today's professional works for a law firm, corporation, clinic, etc. However, the responsibility for his or her action belong and return ultimately to themselves as individuals.

But like the samurai or the officer after the development of the centralized nation state, the individual professional is most often unable to effectively alter the course of the society or organization he or she serves. As a lawyer, I cannot begin to tell you how many times I have had to defend people or organizations I could not stand, or, adopt positions that I felt were nonsense as a result of my professional responsibilities. I'm sure doctors facing insurance companies and the possibilities of malpractice feel the same way. We are all *ronin*. The rules by which we are supposed to operate are opaque, contradictory, politically changeable, and more often than not, inapplicable. Nonetheless, as professionals, we must continue to practice.

This is precisely why the martial model is so apropos for professionals. To be human means that one by definition cannot control everything or, for that matter, most things. The world of "things" and other persons, resist. The world, however, is not simply passive and inert. It is also active and expresses forces of its own. Life becomes in this context, very much like the game of chess between the knight and Death in Bergman's film *The Seventh Seal*. Death, however, is just one aspect of the "other" which we find in the world. The "other," the collective forces acting against us, we call Fate. Confucius used the term *Ming*. *Ming* means all and everything over which we have no control. Since *Ming* encompasses so much of our world, we have to arrive at some creative way to exercise our personal freedom in the face of fate. Art is the result of the exercise of freedom in the face of *Ming*. A species of art is ethics. This position is common to both the Ancient Greeks and the samurai thinkers such as Mishima and Jocho. Ethics, according to these thinkers, must in addition to expressing freedom, be beautiful. Beauty is the expression of grace, which is a term for economy of movement and reserve of energy in action. To express beauty and to behave ethically, therefore, one must learn and constantly practice how to act gracefully.

Because of the pervasiveness of *Ming*, one can never be sure of the results of one's actions. This is also an insight derived from the martial way of life. We are limited beings existing with a limited amount of time. Death is always immanent and, our decisions and actions are continually and relentlessly narrowing the possibilities for the freedom remaining in our present lives. Confucius argues, therefore, that ethics is an end in itself. One should do one's very best for others simply for the sake of the beauty of the action itself. One should be gracious. This is also the attitude of the samurai and, of the Christian knight. One must constantly expect to die before seeing the *results* of an action. Therefore, one *has* only the pleasure of the action itself. Life is truly art for art's sake.

The artists of the world have dedicated their lives to this outlook. In the East, Zen in Japan has strongly influenced the intuitive technique of her poets and painters. The works of art produced are done after great concentration, in an instant. A few terse, compact lines; a single brush stroke expressing all. In the West, the movement to more minimalist and abstract forms expresses the same position. The professional, however, fails to understand his or her life and professional expression as a work of art. Therefore, there is dissatisfaction, alcoholism, drug abuse, and cynicism about the professions both from without in the general populace, and from within, from the practitioners themselves. How many lawyers tell self-deprecating lawyer jokes? How many doctors have gotten so caught up in the triple or quadruple booking of appointments, that the pursuit of making the "nut" has crowded out the beauty of healing and led to self-doubt, loathing, and self-medication?

Things may very well have been much clearer when professionals were, in fact, priests. However, modern life and its accompanying secular philosophy have again uncovered the fact that guidance must come from within and that all else is a sham. We are all creative artists, and as such must face the fact that there is no guidance for a creator. Copying is not creation and is, ultimately, doomed to failure.

The professional is an artist. He or she is given a situation; a set of facts. The facts represent *Ming*. They are simply given. A client is rear-ended by a truck and has a whiplash injury. A child has fallen and has a hairline fracture of the tibia. The professional has the knowledge and the training to work with these facts. That is what his or her profession has provided. What he or she does; how he or she applies this professionalism to the facts, is his or her own creation. No two cases are ever the same. Each treatment, each argument, is a work of art. It may be bad or sloppy art, but it is art nonetheless.

The practice of a profession is the continuing education in elegance; grace. My first legal job was as a clerk for a municipal judge. I was in the top ten percent of my class at that time and pretty hot stuff — I thought. I thought that until the first actual criminal court file was tossed on my desk. As I pulled out the various documents, I had no earthly idea what they were! The bailiff and the judge's secretary had to tell me. It was humiliating — and necessary.

After fourteen years of practice, I can prepare for a criminal jury trial in an afternoon. I can be a warm body at a probation hearing on five minutes notice. This is not because I do a slipshod job, but because after fourteen years of practice, I know where the jugular is.

There is a lawyer joke that I love: A man and his lawyer are out hiking in the woods. They turn a corner and run smack into a crouching mountain lion. The lawyer calmly starts taking off his gear. The man asks perplexedly what the lawyer is doing. The lawyer replies, "I'm getting ready to run." To which the exasperated man responds, "Are you nuts? You can't outrun a mountain lion." The lawyer answers, "I know I can't outrun a mountain lion, but all I have to do is outrun you." Every lawyer I've ever told that story to has heartily appreciated it. The long and continuous practice of a profession leads to economy of motion and a preservation of energy. Grace. One learns from experience what is important and what not to waste one's energy on.

One of my first trials was before another municipal court judge. I represented a psychologist who had been giving a couple an extensive series of marriage counseling. The husband was supposed to pay, but after running up a $1200 bill, his wife left him and he refused to pay.

As a green attorney, I felt I had to document each ses-

▶ ▶

sion, each bill, each attempted collection so when the judge asked if I was prepared as plaintiff to proceed, I plopped two and a half feet of documents on my counsel's table. The judge called both attorneys to the side-bar. He informed me that he had no intention of listening to all of that evidence and stated that he would give my client $600. The judge was the sole trier of fact in this case. I can take a hint. $600 is a lot better than nothing. The other attorney was no slouch either. $600 was a lot better than $1200. We settled. Everyone was happy. One learns quickly and through experience just what is important and what is not worth the effort.

When we discussed the *Hagakure* of Jocho Yamamoto, and the works of Inazo Nitobi, we were informed that grace and the etiquette that accompanies it were such that, even while doing the most mundane of things, one radiated power. Professionals who have gained respect in their fields also do this. My wife and I have done natural childbirth for both of my sons. Early in her second pregnancy, my wife became very ill from food poisoning, losing weight and fluids rapidly. As a consequence, my son Brian was born several weeks premature. As my wife was in labor in the hospital, I noticed from the fetal monitor that with every contraction the baby's heart rate cut in half. After a few moments of this, the nurses shoved me out of the way and ordered me into surgical scrubs. As I watched the heart rate with growing alarm, I kept asking the nurses if things were going to be all right. They blew me off, which only added to my terror. I actually started asking myself how I was going to hold my wife together when the baby died. Then I wondered who would hold me together.

Our pediatrician had been called since the baby was in distress. When Dr. Shah arrived, he had a very scared lawyer on his hands, but he strolled in smiling and humming. He talked to me for a moment and radiated such calm that my fears disappeared. My son was born normally and Dr. Shah took over. Before I knew it, I was staring at my second boy sleeping peacefully in an incubator. And strangely enough, I was calm. Grace. Elegance. The power that comes from years of practice.

So we are trained. We practice, and, hopefully gain in grace and power. Again, however, why the discouragement in so many professional people? Once again, the answer must be the concentration on the results of our efforts; the failure to realize that we can control our actions, but *Ming* controls the results. The greatest enemy of the professional, just like any other human being, is self-deception. We cannot control the results of our actions and we cannot even control our clients or patients.

I wish I had a dollar for every client who I carefully advised and for whom I prescribed a well-planned and well-executed legal strategy only to have it completely ignored, having exactly all of the dire predictions I made come true when it was ignored, and then having the client angry at me because things turned out exactly as I said they would.

The client who bribed a witness in the case I described in Chapter Two, for whom I resuscitated a cold case, and who got to a jury despite the opposition of one of the largest and most talented law firms in our area — wanted to sue me because I (not him, he who bribed a witness and neglected his court documents until the final hours before dismissal) lost his case for him! Every lawyer I know meets a client and invariably wonders whether this one will sue for malpractice if the case doesn't go his or her way. Every doctor probably feels the same way. The client ignores your advise. The patient refuses to take his or her medicine. But it's all your fault. We cannot control the results of our action. To think that we can and to concentrate on those results, whether they be victory in trial, a complete cure, or the fee that we will make — is self-delusion and can only lead to unhappiness.

So what is to be done? We have no control and, as professionals, are, in the last analysis, alone. The first thing to be observed is that we have to recognize that there are no rules per se. Rules and laws are for the least intelligent of us, and even then, they don't work. We have dealt at length with the fallacy of attempting to apply rules to human conduct. Advice also cannot be given and very much for the same reason. Instead, as noted in the works on the life of the samurai and the treatises on chivalry, which we have discussed, we can only give an *agenda*, an attitude, feelings. We must get ourselves in a *frame of mind* and proceed, individually, from there. To get into this state of mind, we must recognize a number of points.

First and foremost, we must recognize and acknowledge, if only to ourselves, that life is conflict. We can and will never be satisfied. If an attorney wins a big case, three more will follow. If a doctor saves a life, he or she will inevitably lose one. The house in the country will have leaky window wells. The Jaguar will be in the shop. You will write the perfect contract, but the other guy's attorney will find a loophole. And, finally, even if everything, perhaps especially if everything, is going well, you will sit up in the middle of the night in your bathrobe in your den and wonder "Is this it? Is this what I really want?"

As a human being, and simply as a human being, the truth is that the struggle will never end. To believe otherwise is to delude oneself. This truth is even more pronounced for professionals. Not only do they face the everyday struggles and disappointments of the average person, but, the professions are by definition, conflict oriented. Without a disturbance in the regular course of events, the professional is superfluous. It is only when things go wrong that the professional is assured of getting paid.

As we have stated repeatedly in this book, the profession that by its nature most directly faces continuous conflict is that of the warrior. We have followed the development of the warrior from the rough and tumble days of the barbarians through the knights and samurai, ending with the conversion of the martial outlook into *budo*. This acceptance and embracing of continual conflict makes one continually cognizant and critical of one's skills. It gives an impetus towards perfection, since one realizes that one's survival, as a samurai, as a lawyer, as a doctor, or as a middle-manager, depends upon one's individual skill.

The second thing that one must recognize is that we are alone, as people, and, even more so as professionals. No one does a trial exactly like I do. No one else makes that walk into the courtroom and sweats out the verdict but me. If I make a mistake, no one else gets sued for malpractice but me. This is the same situation as that of the samurai or knight. In battle, if your opponent swings a sword faster and more sure than you, you and only you will die from the blow. This feeling of isolation raises the corollary enunciated by Jocho and Mishima; the way of the samurai is death.

We are limited beings. We cannot be or do everything. We cannot predict the future. We have only a limited and finite amount of time. Using Mishima's analogy, we start from a wide circle of possibilities. As Sartre noted, however, every action and every choice makes the next ring in the cone smaller. This continues throughout life until the final point is reached. We must acknowledge that death is our constant companion.

Again, however, taking our lead from the professional warrior, we must understand that our isolation and our relationship with death brings certain gifts with them. The insight that we are alone and limited gives the possibility and the depth of *feeling* to *appreciate* things. How many of us, when we are young especially, just waste time? We are unconscious. We do not see or hear. Without appreciation, there can be no art. Without the possibility of art, there can be no ethics.

I've noticed that before a particularly serious and important trial, my sensations are heightened. It is as if time slows down. Perhaps this is a chemical reaction brought on by stress, or, in *Qi Gong* theory, a heightening of the energy level and flow. Whatever the reason, the intensity of the moment makes appreciation possible, and with appreciation comes tolerance and compassion. We tend to want to think of the professional warrior as a gruff, callous individual, inured to all "softness." However, that is not what is revealed in our readings of the works of both samurai and knights. Our Japanese authors speak of "the tenderness of the samurai" as a natural and assumed expression of the martial temperament. Of course it is natural that these people have the greatest appreciation of life of all of humankind. The knowledge of death without appreciation is simply fear. The recognition of one's isolation and limitations gives one the possibility of appreciation and compassion. It also frees one to act.

If we know that we will ultimately cease to exist in this life, and, if we learn to appreciate every moment intensely, we realize that the most intense feelings we can have come from the impression of our freedom on the world. These feelings come from creation; from action. In the last analysis we only have our actions. To think that we have anything else is yet another delusion.

Perhaps the greatest and most intense feeling, finally, is the feeling of our own power and energy. This is the insight not only of Nietzsche and the *Qi Gong* Masters, but of the ancients who coined their words for virtue from terms relating to biological, sexual potency and energy. It is good to feel one's power. This brings us to our final recognition. We all have virtue.

The ancient Chinese sages, but especially Mencius, asserted specifically that human beings are originally good. We all have the "beginnings" or roots of virtue in us. But these roots must be developed. When they are developed, they flower naturally, as the Taoists posited, in good fruit. That is, in a beautiful and ethical world.

What conclusions can we draw from these insights? Life is conflict, we face this struggle alone with the clock running, and, we all have the potential, the power to express ourselves, to create in this context. There are two basic conclusions, that of the Taoists and that of the Confucians.

We are alone, in conflict, and we are armed. To face the conflict, we must develop ourselves, perfect ourselves as much as possible. This is called "self-cultivation" and is the goal of Confucian philosophy. How do we cultivate ourselves? By following nature, as the Taoists decree.

The picture that most of us get from the idea of concentration on oneself and the following of nature in our present society, however, is that of a self-absorbed, egotistical lout having sex in the punch bowl because nature called. This only shows how far we have strayed *from* nature. Humans have spent the bulk of their history perverting and manipulating nature, and then presenting the tramp that has been produced as the original article. These layers of "civilized" gunk must be stripped away, much like the muscular armor that Wilhelm Reich excised in his psychotherapy. This is also the position of the Taoists, who proclaim that one must learn to forget and must cease carving the block so as to return to the original purity of one's nature.

But how does one, especially a professional with the intense competition of professional life, do this?

First one must, like the Taoists, learn to forget. Forget about your fees. Forget about the vacation home on the lake. Forget about your opponent. Forget about your doubts. The only opponent is yourself. You do not face trials, operations, or rival firms selling another brand of toothpaste. You face Zen *koans*; the nonsense riddles that have no answer and drive you to distraction. As you face the *koans* presented by your practice, you must observe that the tensions around and in you rise. So does the energy or virtue in you. You must learn to observe and feel this energy.

As with *Qi Gong* practice and Zen meditation, at first the virtue will not *speak* to you. That is when you must give it an opening. You have a choice: you can go nuts and raise a wonderful, world-class ulcer, or, you can become a better, stronger warrior. Use the energy rather than ignore it or find it a distraction. Tension is good. It makes one strong. If channeled correctly it can prepare you for battle.

The next thing to do after recognizing and getting the "feel" of one's virtue or energy is to learn how to channel it. This can be done in any number of ways. These ways are actually *do*. Every person has a *do*. That is how it is possible for masters to arise. A master creates him or herself. This creation is as unique as anything by Degas, Monet, Picasso, etc. But one must start on the path somewhere. It can and should be in one's profession, but traditional *do* training or meditation practice would give one the structure, the "form" that could be carried over to one's profession. In doing this, trials, operations, sales presentations, become *kata*. Practicing *kata* leads to perfection. And self-perfection is all that any of us can own.

I can hear many of my colleagues saying, in a rather cynical manner, that this is all fine and good, but will it make me a better lawyer, surgeon, salesman, or manager? The answer is yes, and in ways not envisioned by those asking the question.

The term "better" has two meanings. In the first sense, it means "more skillful," more likely to win. Therefore, more likely to make a bundle. The second meaning is "more ethical," "more moral," a better person.

Concerning the first meaning of "better," constant practice and intense self-criticism cannot help but make one's skills more proficient. However, to stop there, as the *budo* masters observe, is to limit oneself unduly and by so doing, prepare oneself for ultimate failure and defeat. The mere technician has always been despised by the martial philosophers, both Eastern, like Jocho, and, Western, like Lull and Charny. Who does the greatest swordsman in Spain fear? The second greatest swordsman in Spain? No, because he already knows what his rival is capable of. He knows already how to counter him. That is why one is first and one is second. The greatest swordsman in Spain lies awake at night fearing the kid who comes from nowhere, out of the provinces, and fights in a new and unconventional manner. Such a unique and threatening situation can only be met by one who has mastered more than an artificial technique.

The martial philosophers are united in asserting that it is the *total* person, the total, unique samurai or knight, who is of interest and who is worthy of his or her title. Which brings us naturally to the second meaning of "better." We have seen that the adoption of the martial view of life naturally brings with it an intense sense of individuality and an appreciation of the uniqueness of existence. This appreciation extends not only to material things such as paintings, sculptures, or teacups, but most especially to human beings. Too often our more noetic forms of religion and law tell us through their laws and commandments to love one another. The proof that general, ungrounded directives don't work is in the mere fact that there are ten commandments, not to mention the millions of pages of positive laws and statutes. Jesus gave one commandment: Love one another. If external directives were feasible, that single commandment would be quite sufficient.

Because the warrior faces death continually, an appreciation of a limited life leads him or her to feelings of compassion. The warrior, more than anyone, appreciates the sadness and promise of this limited existence. Therefore, he or she respects other human beings. He or she will do his or her duty, and even cause death if necessary, but will never take this lightly. When one goes beyond mere technique, one sees that the taking of life, or for that matter, the hurting either physically or emotionally, of another human being is not something as superficial as the violent and ignorant fare we see constantly portrayed in the movies.

From this desire not to hurt anyone comes etiquette. It is no accident that etiquette and the respect for politeness and manners are most developed in cultures such as that of Japan, in which the martial spirit is most pervasive.

Love one another. Confucius said that *jen* or human-heartedness encompasses all of the virtues. The Confucians believed that it was human nature to form relationships, that the nature of the human being was love. This is also the position of Wilhelm Reich and Alexander Lowen. When you are in love, you will deny yourself in order to give your utmost for your beloved. Again, this is reflected in the romantic and courtly love so highly valued by the samurai and by European chivalry. By drawing one's energy away from the perversions and distractions of life, and, of one's career, and by concentrating and directing it through the following of a *do*, one's energy will express itself in the only way it can — naturally. We must trust this natural expression because, as the Chinese philosophers state, it is good and motivated by love.

Will the practicing of a *do* make you a better person in the sense of more ethical or moral? Yes, of course.

Since I have begun studying Chinese and especially Confucian philosophy, I have often wondered what a world in which everyone spent their energies on self-cultivation would be like. My studies of the theories of Wilhelm Reich have given me psychological and biological clues. If indeed, as Mencius asserts, we are all originally good, and I believe our studies of virtue and bioenergetics demonstrate that we are, then the uncovering and freeing of this original nature can only make the world a better place. It is true, of course, that we will always be at the mercy of the forces of *Ming* or fate. The girl or boy we love may not love us. The trial that we needed to win will go the other way. The patient will die. Confucius knew this and started from it. However, by controlling ourselves, we will only grown in strength, comprehension, and, incidentally, technique. We will in short, be better.

As a corollary, a world or society in which people minded their own business and tended to their own natures would certainly be a better place. There would be no horrendous loss of energy trying to make rule after rule, law after law, which due to human nature, would always and everywhere fail. The only purpose of such external appendages is to artificially gratify someone's sense of power and control and to delude the perpetrator into believing that they are *making* people better.

Ethical behavior comes from within. It is individual and unique. It is the product of one's virtue or bioenergy. The conscious growth and direction of this energy creates a work of art — one's character. If properly cultivated, this character will express grace and beauty. One will be a person capable of ethical acts.

For myself, I do not seriously believe that most people in our current society, with its perversions and unnatural motivations, can create and follow their own *dos*. For most of us I would strongly recommend finding a teacher of a *do* that appeals to you intuitively. For those wishing to read on this subject I would recommend the works of Dr. Yang Jwing-Ming, Master Ni Hua Ching, or Mantak Chia, who are mentioned and discussed in my previous book, *The Tao of Bioenergetics*. Do not study your *do* for technique. Do not study karate to beat up the guy in the bar. Do not study the tea ceremony to pour tea. The focus on results is a mistake. Self-delusion implies self-division and a radical depletion of your energy or virtue. The *do* is an arrow that flies in a straight path and pins your heart into your chest.

Concluding Remarks

As a philosophy major in college, my main interests were in the areas of metaphysics, aesthetics, and, to a lesser extent, epistemology. The type of philosophical inquiry that interested me least was ethics and moral philosophy. I found it generally morbid and dull, and had a sneaking suspicion that what passed for moral philosophy was a sham. Accordingly, you can readily understand that I had no desire to write a book on ethics.

Nonetheless, as I have watched our society unfold over the brief period of my life, I have seen an inexorable and irresistible lowering of the intelligence, taste, and morality of my own people. In many discussions with other mid-forties types like myself, I have found that we all remember what it was like for Americans growing up in the years after World War II. During the years from 1945-1973, all of us had a sense of optimism. That is not to say that we agreed on everything. Obviously, our history speaks otherwise. However, the underlying assumption for all of us was that if there was a problem, we, as Americans, could fix it. Be it poverty, Communism, civil rights, whatever; give us the facts, let us tinker around and we could fix it. We were, after all, Americans.

Over the past twenty-odd years, we have lost that faith. It's a loss of faith in our country, our society, and, most importantly, in ourselves. I did not wish to write a book on ethics and quite frankly, I'm not sure that I have. I do not believe that ethics is possible. I do wholeheartedly believe, however, that human goodness is.

I base this belief on the philosophers, depth-psychologists, and warriors whom we have studied. Plato, through Socrates' mouth, stated that all learning is just remembering what we already know. This, in many ways, is also the insight of Confucius, Mencius, and the Taoist sages. We must remember that we as human beings are naturally good. There are far too many people, especially in public places today, who tell us otherwise. They are liars and they hate and despise their own humanity. They hate themselves.

I do not think it is possible to write a book of ethics since ethics, in the form of rules, laws, or even principles cannot exist. What can exist, and what I think I have uncovered, at least somewhat, are natural processes or procedures that allow one to uncover and express the goodness that is inside of all human beings. Virtue makes life good, not necessarily "moral" in the perjorative sense of that word.

The procedures that I have extolled in this book are those of the martial forms, or *budo*. Americans never wanted world leadership. It fell to us by default in August of 1945. We have frantically repeated the mistakes of our European, especially our British, predecessors as world leaders. Looking outside, we have come to this point. I am not an isolationist, but I believe that it is time to look within; to our own energy, genesis, and yes, history. Copying is not creation. Human beings must create. By nature. The Republic must be capable of self-renewal or the Republic will fail. The citizen of the Republic must cultivate him or herself and recall and listen to his or her human nature, or democracy in America will become just another "thing."

I have stated repeatedly in this book that copying is not creativity. However, while this is true, it is acceptable to take raw material from other sources. Since colonial times when the West came into sustained contact with the East, translations of Eastern thought and practices have steadily been appearing in the West. Many educated Westerners have responded enthusiastically to this material and have imitated the exotic practices found therein.

Imitation, however, is mindless and self-defeating. As the

thought and arts of Asia (or Africa and Native America for that matter) become more and more accesible in Western countries, it can only be hoped that the Westerner will use his or her own unique cultural perspective in working with and through these other cultural artifacts.

Budo, bushido, and *Qi Gong* are artifacts of Asian wisdom. That does not mean that they cannot be owned and honored by Westerners. What it does mean is that Westerners cannot approach these diciplines as Easterns do, but rather from their own free cultural heritage. Freedom united with the given is art. The synthesis of East and West provides a seminal opportunity for a universal, human aesthetic — and ethic.

NOTES

1. Carl Jung, *Mysterium Coniunctionis* Bollingen Series XX, (Princeton University Press: New York, 1963), xvi-xvii; Carl Jung, *On Psychic Energy* Bollingen Series XX, vol. 8 (Princeton University Press: New York, 1966), 26-27, 32-35.
2. Ibid., pp. 4, 18-22, 24-5; Roger Trigg, *Ideas of Human Nature, An Historical Introduction* (Basil Blackwell, LTD: Oxford and New York, 1988), 140-142.
3. Jung, *Energy*, 32-35.
4. Trigg, 60-61.
5. Ibid.
6. Ibid.
7. Ibid., 63-65.
8. Ibid.
9. Ibid, 57.
10. Ibid., 57-58.
11. Frederick Copleston, S.J., *A History of Philosophy* Vol. 3, Part II (Image Books, Doubleday and Company, Inc: Garden City, New York, 1963), 130-132.
12. Fung Yu-Lan, *A Short History of Chinese Philosophy* (The Free Press: New York and London, 1948), 160.
13. Trigg, 58.
14. Jung, *Energy,* 19-22; Carl Jung, *The Undiscovered Self* (Mentor Books, New American Library, Times Mirror: New York and Toronto, 1957), 11-27; See generally, Wilhelm Reich, *The Mass Psychology of Fascism* (Farrar, Straus and Giroux: New York, 1970).
15. Donn F. Draeger, *Classical Budo* (Weatherhill: New York and Tokyo, 1973), 13-16.
16. Maurice Keen, *Chivalry* (Yale University Press: New Haven and London, 1984), 206-207.
17. Ibid., 30, 91, 117, 238.
18. Inazo Nitobe, *Bushido* The Soul of Japan (Charles E. Tuttle and Company, Inc: Rutland, Vt. and Tokyo, 1969), 13-16; Keen, 14.
19. Ludwig Wittgenstein, "Games and Definitions," in *A Modern Book of Aesthetics,* ed., Melvin Rader (Holt, Rinehart, and Winston: New York, 1962), 195-199.
20. Draeger, 36.
21. Ibid., 42.
22. Ibid., 52-53, 61, 65.
23. Copleston, op. cit., Vol. 6, Part I
24. Ibid., 238-239, ed. William L. Kelly, S.J. and Andrew Tallon, *Readings In The Philosphy of Man* (McGraw-Hill Book Company : New York, 1967, 1972), 68.
25. Ibid., 61; Trigg, 69; ed., Leslie Stevenson, *The Study of Human Nature* (Oxford University Press: New York and Oxford, 1981), 111.
26. Fung, 1, 4, 6.
27. Trigg, 7; John Burnet, *Early Greek Philosophy* (Meridian Books, The World Publishing Company : Cleveland and New York, 1957), 335.
28 See; Bertrand Russell, *The ABC of Relativity* (Mentor Books, New American Library, Times Mirror: New York, 1958); Michael Talbott, *Mysticism and The New Physics* (Bantam Books: Toronto, London, New York, 1981).

29. Bertrand Russell, *A History of Western Philosophy* (Clarion Books, Simon and Schuster: New York, 1945), 73.
30. Ibid., 108.
31. Ibid., 149.
32. Ibid., 121-122, 128; Copleston, op. cit., Vol. I, Part I, 69-70, 202.
33. Russell, *History*, 122-125.
34. Copleston, op. cit., Vol. I, Part I, 192; Stevenson, 40.
35. Copleston, op. cit., Vol. 1, Part I, 189.
36. Russell, *History,* 139; Trigg, 11, Stevenson, 38, 40; Kelly, 1.
37. Ibid; Stevenson, 40; Trigg, 12, 15, Russell, *History*, 137-138.
38. Trigg, 13-14; Stevenson, 40, 49, 52, 57-59.
39. Trigg, 22-23; Stevenson, 66, 68.
40. Trigg, 40; Stevenson, 68.
41. Trigg, 29-30; Stevenson, 66.
42. Trigg, 30-32,40; Stevenson, 68.
43. Ibid., 73, Russell, *History*, 284-285.
44. Trigg, 41, 43-44; Stevenson, 73; Kelly, 33, 36.
45. Trigg, 38-39, 43-44; Stevenson, 73; Kelly, 33, 36, 38.
46. Russell, *History*, 560, 565.
47. Ibid., 564; Kelly, 43.
48. Copleston, op. cit., Vol 4, 129; Stevenson, 81.
49. Ibid.; Kelly, 47, Copleston, op. cit., Vol. 4, 144-146.
50. Ibid., 28-29.
51. Ibid., 109-111; Kelly, 45-46.
52. Copleston, op. cit. Vol. 4, 28.
53. Russell, History, 609; Kelly, 49.
54. Ibid., p. 51; Copleston, op. cit., Vol. 5, Part I, 101-102.
55. Kelly, p. 54; Copleston, op. cit., Vol. 5, Part II, 21.
56. Ibid., 27-28.
57. Ibid., p. 106; Kelly, p. 61
58. Jeremy M. Hayward, *Shifting Worlds, Changing Minds, Where the Sciences and Buddhism Meet* (New ScienceLibrary, Shambala: Boston and London, 1987), 58; Stevenson, 17,21.
59. Kelly, 68; Copleston, op. cit., Vol. 6, Part II, 8-9, 36-39.
60. Ibid., 8-9; Kelly, 68.
61. Copleston, op. cit., 62.
62. Russell, *History,* 731-732.
63. Ibid.
64. Ibid., 733; Kelly, 84-86.
65. Ibid., 90-92, Russell, *History*, 755.
66. Kelly, 108-113.
67. Trigg., 122, 125-126; Kelly, 115.
68. Stevenson, 193.
69. Ibid., 211-212.
70. Kelly, 139, 174, 225, 229; Stevenson, 267-271, 294, 296.
71. Kelly, 232.
72. Stevenson, 274; Kelly, 224.
73. Kelly, 214.
74. Ibid., 242.
75. Ibid., 233-234.
76. Ibid., 243.
77. Ibid.
78. George A. Katchmer, Jr., *The Tao of Bioenergetics* (YMAA Publications: Boston, 1993), 112.
79. Ed. S. Radhakrishnan and T. Raju, *The Concept of Man, A Study in*

Comparative Philosophy (Johnson Publishing Company : Lincoln, NB, 1060), 211.
80. Ibid.
81. Pandit Rajmani Tigunait, *Seven Systems of Indian Philosophy* (The Himalayan International Institute of Science, Yoga and Philosophy in the USA: Honesdale, PA., 1983), 10.
82. Ibid., 13.
83. Ibid.
84. Ibid., 15; Radhakrishnan, 212-214.
85. Ibid., 245; Tigunait, 26; Chandradkhar Sharma, *A Critical Study of Indian Philosophy* (Rider and Company : London, Melbourne, Sidney, Auckland, Bombay, Toronto, Johannesburg, New York, 1960), 13.
86. Tigunait, 15; Radhakrishnan, 212.
87. Ibid., 213.
88. Tigunait, 18-26.
89. Radhakrishnan, 214-215.
90. Ibid.
91. Ibid.
92. Sharma, 19.
93. Ibid., 25.
94. Ibid., 21-23.
95. Ibid.
96. Ibid.
97. Ibid., 24.
98. Ibid., 24-25.
99. Radhakrishnan, 217.
100. Ibid.
101. Ibid.
102. Tigunait, 154, Radhakrishnan, 231, Sharma, 34.
103. Ibid., 128.
104. Radhakrishnan, 208; Sharma, generally.
105. Ibid.
106. Ibid.
107. Ibid.
108. Ibid.
109. Fung, 20.
110. Fung, 301.
111. See generally, Katchmer, Chapters Four and Five.
112. Ibid.
113. Ibid., Chapter Five.
114. Ibid.
115. Fung, 1.
116. Ibid., 69.
117. Ibid., 70.
118. Ibid., 143.
119. Ibid., 144.
120. Ibid.
121. Ibid., 160.
122. See generally, William G. Ouchi, *Theory Z, How American Business Can Meet the Japanese Challenge* (Avon: New York, 1981).
123. Ibid., 58-59.
124. Ibid., generally.
125. Fung, 191, 205, 212-213.
126. Ibid., 100-101, 105.
127. Ibid., 100.

128. Ibid., 105-106.
129. Ibid., 112.
130. Ibid., 103.
131. Ibid., 218.
132. Jung, *Energy,* 32-35.
133. See generally, Lynn Thorndike, *A History of Magic and Experimental Science* (MacMillan: New York, 1923-1958).
134. See, Friedrick Nietzsche, *On The Genealogy of Morals* (Vintage Books: New York, 1966), Kelly, 115.
135. Copleston, op. cit., Vol. 5, Part II, 87.
136. Kelly, 62-63.
137. Ibid., 66.
138. Richard Von Mises, *Positivism* (Dover Publications, Inc: New York, 1951), 205-218.
139. Stevenson, 307-308.
140. Katchmer, 33.
141. Doris Chase Doane and King Keyes, *How to Read Tarot Cards* (Funk and Wagnall's: New York, 1967), 88-92.
142. Ibid., generally.
143. See generally, Hans Jonas, *The Gnostic Religion, The Message of the Alien God and The Beginnings of Christianity* (Beacon Press: Boston, 1958).
144. Oscar Wilde, "The Critic as Artist," *The Complete Works of Oscar Wilde* (Perennial Library, Harper and Row: (Grand Rapids, New York, Philadelphia, St. Louise, San Francisco, London, Singapore, Sydney, Tokyo, 1966), 1009-1060.
145. Nitobe, 15-16.
146. John Meskill, ed., *An Introduction to Chinese Civilization* (D.L. Heatham Company : Lexington, MA., Toronto, London, 1973), 561.
147. W. Scott Morton, *Japan, Its History and Culture* (Thomas Y. Crowell Company : New York, 1970), 17-35.
148. Ibid.
149. Fung, 166.
150. Ch'u Chai and Winberg Chai, *Confucianism* (Barron's Educational Series, Inc: New York, 1973), 37.
151. Daisetz T. Suzuki, *Zen and Japanese Culture* (Pantheon Books: New York, 1959), 39-59.
152. Chai, 39.
153. Chai, 38.
154. Ibid.
155. Ibid., 40-41.
156. Fung, 45.
157. Ibid.
158. Fung, 42.
159. Jung, *Energy,* 32-35.
160. Fung, 9, 38-40, 45.
161. Ibid., 9.
162. See generally, Yang Jwing-Ming, *The Roof of Chinese Chi Kung* (YMAA Publication Center: Boston, 1989).
163. Ibid., 60.
164. Fung, 45.
165. D. Simpson, comp., *Cassell's New Compact Latin Dictionary* (Dell Publishing Company, Inc: New York, 1963), "Virtus," "Vir."
166. Chai, 38-40; Fung, 45.
167. Cassell's, "Virtus."
168. Ibid., "*Vis.*"

169. New Catholic Encyclopedia, Vol. XIV (McGraw-Hill Company : New York, 1967), "Virtue."
170. See generally, Sigmund Freud, *The Interpretation of Dreams* (Avon Books: New York, 1965, originally 1905).
171. Carl Jung, *Symbols of Transformation*, Bolliggen Series XX (Princeton University Press: New York, 1956), 258.
172. Carl Jung, *Mysterium*, 113, 288-289; Mandala *Symbolism*, Bollingen Series XX (Princeton University Press: Princeton, 1959, 1969, 1972), 48, 51.
173. Katchmer, 9.
174. Ibid., 157-189.
175. New Catholic Encyclopedia, Vo. XIV, "Virtue."
176. Ibid.
177. Ibid.
178. Kelly, 90.
179. Trigg, 125.
180. Ibid., 125-126, 129.
181. See generally, Jack J. Spector, *The Aesthetics of Freud, A Study in Psychoanalysis and Art* (McGraw-Hill Book Company: New York, St. Louis, San Francisco, Dusseldorf, Mexico, Montreal, Panama, Sao Paulo, Toronto 1972).
182. Friedrich Nietzsche, *Beyond Good and Evil* (Vintage Books: New York, 1966), 204-208.
183. Ibid., Kelly, 128.
184. See eg., Luke 8:14, Mark 10:17-27.
185. My source for this story is D.W. Griffith's "Orphans of the Storm," in which it occurs and is footnoted as a true event, giving the name of the nobleman involved.
186. Nietzsche, *Good and Evil*, 204-208.
187. Trigg, 125-126, 129.
188. J. E. Zimmerman, *Dictionary of Classical Mythology* (Harper Row: New York, Evanston, London, 1964), "Arete."
189. Freud, *Dreams*, generally.
190. Wilhelm Reich, *The Invasion of Compulsory Sex Morality* (Farrar, Straus and Giroux: New York, 1971), vii.
191. Fung, 231-233.
192. Fung, 62.
193. Ibid., 65
194. Ibid.
195. Ibid., 19.
196. Ibid.
197. Ibid., 19, 64, 165.
198. Katchmer, 8-9.
199. Ibid.
200. Fung, 21, 177.
201. Ibid., 42.
202. Ibid.
203. Katchmer, 15; Chai, 14.
204. Fung, 77.
205. Ibid., 70.
206. Ibid., 42.
207. Ibid., 43.
208. Ibid., 160.
209. Ibid., 70.
210. Ibid., 77.

▶ ▶

211. Ibid., 21.
212. Ibid., 238.
213. William DeBary, *Neo-Confucian Orthodoxy and the Learning of Mind-and-Heart* (Columbia University: New York, 1981), xv-xvi.
214. Ibid.
215. Ibid.
216. Fung, 273-275.
217. Ibid., 298-9, 301.
218. Ibid., 301.
219. Ibid., 302-303.
220. Chai, 37.
221. Carl Jung, *Energy*, 32-35.
222. Nitobe, 15.
223. Nitobe, ix, xii, 8.
224. Ibid., 7.
225. Ibid., 7-8.
226. Ibid., 4.
227. Ibid.
228. Ibid., 5.
229. Ibid., 6.
320. Ibid.
231. Ibid., 11-16.
232. Ibid., 11-12.
233. Ibid., 14.
234. Ibid.
235. Ibid., 15-16.
236. Ibid., 17.
237. Ibid.
238. Ibid., 73.
239. Ibid., 74.
240. Ibid., 42.
241. Ibid., 49.
242. Ibid., 23-25.
243. Ibid., 36, 26.
244. Ibid., 26-27.
245. Ibid., 25-26.
246. Ibid., 26.
247. Ibid., 27.
248. Ibid.
249. Ibid., 37.
250. Ibid., 36.
251. Ibid., 50.
252. Arthur Koestler, *The Lotus and the Robot* (MacMillan: New York, 1961), 220.
253. Nitobe, 50.
254. Ibid., 55-56.
255. Ibid., 55.
256. Ibid.
257. Ibid., 54.
258. Ibid.
259. Yukio Mishima, *The Way of the Samurai, Yukio Mishima on Hagakure in Modern Life* (Basic Books, Inc: New York, 1977), 90.
260. Ibid., vii, 34.
261. Ibid.
262. Ibid., 8.

263. Ibid., ix, 69.
264. Ibid., 7.
265. Ibid., 39-40.
266. Ibid., ix, 69.
267. Ibid., 39.
268. Ibid., 9.
269. Ibid.
270. Ibid., 33, 42-43.
271. Ibid., 23, 41.
272. Ibid., 24.
273. Ibid., 7, 45, 56, 61, 84.
274. Ibid., 7, 44.
275. Ibid., 46, 49-50.
276. Ibid., 104-105.
277. Ibid., 45, 53.
278. Ibid.
279. Ibid., 44, 69.
280. Ibid., 61.
281. Ibid., 46.
282. Ibid., 54-55.
283. Ibid.
284. Ibid., 81.
285. Ibid., 84-85.
286. Ibid.
287. Ibid., 84.
288. Ibid., 86.
289. Ibid.
290. Nitobe, 4, 160, 182; Mishima, 41.
291. Keen, 2.
292. Ibid.
293. Ibid.
294. Ibid.
295. Ibid., 6, 11.
296. Ibid., 5.
297. Ibid., 6.
298. Ibid., 16; Ramon Lull, *The Book of the Order of Chivalry*, trans., Robert
     Adams (San Houston State University Press: Huntsville, TX., 1991), 28.
299. Keen, 11.
300. Ibid., 11-12.
301. Ibid., 2.
302. Ibid., 25-26.
303. Ibid.
304. Ibid.
305. Ibid.
306. Ibid.
307. Ibid.
308. Ibid., 13.
309. Ibid., 45.
310. Ibid., 46.
311. Ibid., 173-174.
312. Ibid. 85.
313. Ibid.
314. Ibid., 87.
315. Ibid, 83-84.
316. Ibid, 88-92.

317. Ibid., 91.
318. Ibid., 14, 91.
319. Ibid., 108-109, 11-112.
320. Ibid., 111-114, 116.
321. Ibid., 121-123.
322. Ibid.
323. Ibid., 222-224.
324. Ibid., 161.
325. Ibid., 146, 161.
326. Ibid.
327. J.F.C. Fuller, *The Conduct of War,* 1789-1961 (Minerva Press: New York, 1961), 34-36.
328. Ibid., 11.
329. Ibid.
330. Ibid.
331. Lull, vii.
332. Ibid.
333. Ibid.; Keen, 11.
334. Lull, 1-2.
335. Ibid., 2.
336. Ibid., 3.
337. Ibid., 6-7.
338. Ibid., 7.
339. Ibid., 11.
340. Ibid., 11-12.
341. Ibid., 13.
342. Ibid., 14.
343. Ibid., 21.
344. Ibid., 21-23, 34.
345. Ibid., 28.
346. Ibid., 31-32.
347. Ibid., 33.
348. Ibid., 79.
349. Ibid.
350. Ibid., 77.
351. Acts 2:3.
352. Keen, 13.
353. Ibid., 57.
354. Ibid., 62-63.
355. Ibid., 69.
356. Ibid., 39; Nitobe, 30.
357. Lull, 33-34.
358. Nitobe, 17.
359. Draeger, 14.
360. Ibid., 17.
361. Ibid., 67.
362. Ibid., 22.
363. Ibid., 22-23.
364. Ibid., 23.
365. Ibid.
366. Ibid.
367. Ibid.
368. Ibid.
369. Ibid., 23-24.
370. Ibid., 24.

371. Ibid.
372. Ibid.
373. Ibid., 25.
374. Ibid.
375. Ibid., 25-28.
376. Ibid., 33.
377. Fuller, 23.
378. Ibid.
379. Dennis M. Campbell, *Doctors, Lawyers, Ministers: Christian Ethics in Professional Practice* (Abingdon: Nashville, 1982), 20-21.
380. Ibid., 19-20.
381. Ibid., 25.
382. Ibid., 25-26.